ON THE
HIGHROAD
— *of* —
SURRENDER

FRANCES J. ROBERTS

BARBOUR
PUBLISHING

DEDICATED IN GRATITUDE

to the faithful saints whose prayers
help sustain me in this ministry of sharing His words.

© 1973 by Frances J. Roberts

ISBN 1-58660-730-8

Cover image © Thinkstock

Library of Congress Cataloging-in-Publication Data

Roberts, Frances J.
    On the highroad of surrender / Frances J. Roberts.
        p. cm.
    ISBN 1-58660-730-8 (pbk.)
    1. Devotional literature. 2. Christian literature. I. Title.

    BV4801.R665 2004
    242—dc22

                                2004004892

Published by Barbour Publishing, Inc., P.O. Box 719, Uhrichsville, Ohio 44683, www.barbourbooks.com

Our mission is to publish and distribute inspirational products offering exceptional value and biblical encouragement to the masses.

 Member of the
Evangelical Christian
Publishers Association

Printed in the United States of America.
5 4 3 2 1

Contents

PREFACE

On the Highroad of Surrender goes forth into the world, born of prayer, and breathed by the Spirit. For it is only the Spirit of God who is able in His infinite wisdom to give us in words His blessed encouragement that we might not faint on this journey of the soul toward the heavenly city.

Bent with weariness, and grieved by his own failures, man grapples with misfortune and looks for the Hand that will lift him out of his despair. In much patience God waits to be that One who is worshipped, praised, and loved with constancy though all hell rise in protest.

Written in true prophetic style, *The Highroad* brings you God's own word to your own heart. To this end we labor, until that day when "we all come in the unity of the faith, and of the knowledge of the Son of God, unto a perfect man, unto the measure of the stature of the fulness of Christ" (Ephesians 4:13).

Many Scripture references have been given. It is not the desire of the author that this book displace God's Holy Word, but that it stimulate a hunger for a deeper appreciation of the Bible, the supreme revelation of all truth.

May His blessing rest upon you, the reader, as you press on to know the riches of God's grace, always looking unto Him who is the author and the finisher of our faith, the Lord Jesus Christ, to whom be all the glory and honor forever.

Amen.

TODAY

TODAY I'll trust Thee, Father God.
Thy hand may hold the chastening rod,
But I will love Thee nonetheless,
As when in pleasure Thou dost bless.

TODAY I'll walk with head held high,
Nor ask to know the reason why
Heart doth break and winds are chill—
Still I pray to do Thy will.

TODAY, Your gift of love and grace,
Let me but look upon Thy face;
Strength of my life, my keeping power,
Be near me in the testing hour.

TODAY I dedicate to Thee;
Thy purpose, Lord, fulfill in me,
That I may say when comes the night:
"This is the path of peace and light."

F J R

Praise Transforms

In every thing give thanks:
for this is the will of God in Christ Jesus concerning you.

1 Thessalonians 5:18

Rejoice in the Lord always, for as you rejoice and give thanks, you release heaven's treasures and shower upon your head the blessings of a delighted Father. Nothing so thoroughly delights the Father's heart as the praises of His children.

For praise exercises the heart toward gratitude, and gratitude nurtures contentment, and you may know for a certainty that no fruit ever appears on the tree of discontent.

So praise, My children, and never cease in your praising, for in the midst of it I will manifest Myself, and you will understand that when I demand of you your praises it is for your highest good.

Out of praises come courage, faith, strength, optimism, clarity, and peace. Out of praises come health and happiness and the soul satisfaction men seek in the world and do not find.

Praise will transform the humblest dwelling to a hallowed haven. It will light the countenance and make the plainest face beautiful. It is impossible for the man who has learned unceasing praise to be a failure. God's blessing attends his path, and God's Spirit rules his heart. He is eternally at peace with both God and man.

IDENTITY

Out of much tribulation I bring forth a people for the glory of My Name. I am shaping you in the furnace of affliction that I may set My seal upon you and display in you My own identity. I desire that you be one with Me in all I have purposed, and as I move in the earth today to redeem the lost and deliver the captives, you are moving with Me whenever your soul and spirit are yielded to Me as an open channel of prayer in the Spirit.

My heart is grieved when those who profess to be My children neglect their intercessory prayer life. They do despite to the spirit of grace by thus neglecting their responsibility toward others. Can a man love God while ignoring the need of his brother? Truly, I say to you, if you confess your love to Me, I test that profession by the degree of genuine concern you exhibit toward others. "If a man love God, let him love his brother also," states the Scripture.

Let your compassion be measured by no lesser standard than the love of Christ for your own soul. Unless your righteousness exceeds that of the hypocrite, you shall not enter in, even as he shall not enter in.

1 JOHN 4:19–21

REJOICE ALWAYS

Knowing that I love you at ALL times will bring comfort in the hours when you need it most. Be obedient to My command that you rejoice in the Lord ALWAYS. It is because I must become your one true source of life and joy that I allow the difficult circumstances to come. In them I test your love for Me. It is not a time for you to test *My love for you!* My love for you is constant and is not to be reckoned by your own happiness or unhappiness. I send all in love. If you have unhappiness, it is because of your own wrong reactions.

Learn to react *rightly,* and properly discern My intention. Never blame Me for your misery, for it is not from My hand.

PSALM 34:1

THE LANGUAGE *of* LOVE

Be silent, My child, and when you speak, let it be your heart that calls My name. Many have My name upon their lips but their hearts are a hollow shell. Love is not in a mouth that is full, but in an overflowing heart.

It is with the HEART man believes unto righteousness, and with the mouth he confesses unto salvation (Romans 10:10). No mouth shall testify of salvation and speak the truth until first the heart has believed unto righteousness.

I listen for the words of your heart. I understand the language of love. He who speaks only with his mouth speaks a language that in heaven is an unknown tongue.

Even so, My child, when you listen for My voice, listen with your HEART. The ear listens with curiosity, but the heart listens with obedience. Be that one who listens with the heart. Be that one who is tuned to the Father's will and understands the language of heaven.

You may miss all that man is saying and still be wise if you converse with Me, for I am the source of all wisdom, and nothing is hidden from My eyes.

PROVERBS 4:23

HEARING *and* DOING

Listen intently for My voice, for you cannot obey Me unless you first HEAR me. However, your ability to hear is sharpened by your desire to be obedient. The functioning of the ear and of the hand are inseparable in the Spirit. They always operate in conjunction with each other. He who HEARS must be also he who DOES what he has heard. Until then, he will not be given a further word.

I am not hiding Myself from the man who does not hear Me. . . . He has cut himself off by self-will and rebellion.

JAMES 1:22

THE SPIRITUAL HOUSE

Over many obstacles I move in the lives of My children,

bringing to pass the full fruition of My plans for each one. Each life is like the building of a house. Much labor is required in preparing the foundation. The most beautiful home will not endure if the foundation is crooked or weak. I build slowly and carefully, and you need patience, for years may pass before the superstructure of your spiritual house begins to take shape.

The swiftness with which I build is determined by your reception of truth. Truth assimilated generates creativity. Obedience practiced generates productivity. Therefore, a teachable spirit and determined desire to do My will hasten the outworking of My purposes in you.

1 CORINTHIANS 3:9–17

RIGHTEOUSNESS, PEACE, *and* JOY

My people shall not languish in weakness, for I will be their strength. They shall not faint by the way, for by My hand will I uphold all them that trust Me.

No evil force can hold back My Spirit, but I will bless and will thrust forth into ministry those who are prepared. Those who are not yet ready, I am purging and chastening so that when they go out it will be in the full provision of My power, and miracles and wonders will manifest as My Word is preached.

Believe Me and trust Me. You need not plot and scheme and plan. All is done already in My eternal now. You will see the fulfillment as you stand firm, not wavering and not striving, for to doubt and to strive is to detain the Spirit. He needs not your help—only your submission. Give it willingly and gladly, yes, give it quickly, for *the kingdom of God is righteousness, peace, and joy in the Holy Ghost,* and you hinder the Spirit when these are not ruling your heart.

ROMANS 14:17–18

ERADICATE DUPLICITY

No true word of prophecy from Me shall be without confirmation. I will make My message very clear to the honest heart. Man would be furthered more in his spiritual life if he spent more time praying that duplicity be eradicated from his heart than by praying to have more truth revealed to him. In most cases, men have already a knowledge of more truth than they are practicing. To add more is of questionable value. To seek further truth before surrendering to the light already received is to invite destruction.

1 JOHN 1:6–10

THE INNER EAR

My commandments are very precious to those who are desirous of doing My will. Those who truly wish to please Me do not seek ways to rationalize and bypass My laws.

My Spirit within a man will cause Him to long with

earnestness to do all I require of him. This very action of seeking
to walk in obedience to the laws of the Spirit opens the inner
ear to hear My voice, and all who hear with the inner ear shall
comprehend in the Spirit, and truth shall be revealed beyond the
surface meaning of the words.

LAMENTATIONS 3:24–26

HARMONY *with the* MESSAGE

I have many glorious things to reveal to you, but you must
pay the price of treasuring, reverencing, and living in harmony
with the message. Truth is always straightforward, and so also
must be the one who receives it, or if he is not already, he must
be willing to be made so.

Man cannot perfect his own righteousness. I must do it for
him, but I need his consent. I need his desire to be made holy.
Surely I will answer when he calls, and I will work in patience
and in gentleness, but I will not stop until the perfecting process
is finished.

PSALM 119:32

ANGELS ASSIST YOU

O My child, do not weep. I am doing a beautiful work.
Stress and pressure and pain are often the path to victory and

understanding. Penitence is a mother to purity, and contrition a father to total consecration.

I am in the midst, and I am a strong deliverer. You need not be concerned. You must not be sad. Courage is the greatest contribution you can make at this point. To be strong now will make the path of recovery easier. Faith is an essential ingredient in every solution. . .often it is the solution itself.

Never underestimate the power of FAITH. Faith is your ability to bring Divine Action to bear upon any given situation. Hold fast. Trust. Unseen angels assist you. Doors are opening to let you pass into safety.

Pour all the intensity of your soul into serving Me, and you will receive great consolation. It is My way provided for your solace and preservation. I will bring you other mercies as I see you have need.

Be strong! I will measure the trials according to your strength and My mercy, but I expect you to stand true. No one can do this FOR you.

It is your supreme hour of destiny. Throw your whole being into winning.

PSALM 30

A MERRY HEART

A merry heart doeth good like a medicine.

PROVERBS 17:22

To mourn adversity multiplies the misfortune. It is not

hypocrisy to rejoice in distress: It is obedience; for, says the Scripture, "REJOICE IN THE LORD ALWAYS"; and again, I say, "REJOICE" (Philippians 4:4). Remember My prophet Habakkuk, who said, "*Although the fig tree shall not blossom, neither shall fruit be in the vines; the labour of the olive shall fail, and the fields shall yield no meat; the flock shall be cut off from the fold, and there shall be no herd in the stalls: Yet I will rejoice in the LORD, I will joy in the God of my salvation. The LORD God is my strength, and he will make my feet like hinds' feet, and he will make me to walk upon mine high places*" (Habakkuk 3:17–19).

Nothing is gained, but much is lost by bitterness of spirit in the day of trouble. You may not be able to escape calamity, but you should even more avoid a doleful countenance because it denotes a tempest in the heart and turbulence of mind and reveals rebellion against the hand of God as it shapes destiny.

Go not in the company of those who magnify evil. Fascination with darkness can be broken by "looking unto Jesus the author and finisher of our faith" (Hebrews 12:2). To Him ought all men look in the hour of desolation. In Him dwelleth only that which is of the light. Peace, joy, and hope are His mantle, and holiness emanates from His presence.

When you are baptized into His Spirit, evil loses its power to destroy you, darkness is dispelled, and the broken spirit healed. Joy is a balm that soothes the soul and lifts the burden from the grieving heart. Joy will be your saving grace, and praise, your meat and drink. Only a joyful heart can worship Me in a way pleasing in My sight.

To weep and mourn is needless waste.

PSALM 71:13–14

THE LAW *of* PLENTY

As poor, yet making many rich;
as having nothing, and yet possessing all things.

2 CORINTHIANS 6:10

Yes, My child, it matters not how little you have of the treasures of the world, for if you are blessed with the bounty of My grace, you shall be always a giver. There is no want for him who is My follower. There is no lack for him who has found that he can buy wine and milk without money and without price (Isaiah 55:1). He has found the law of plenty who has found Me as his source. He shall find abundance crowding his pathway as the blossoms of wildflowers crowd a hillside in springtime.

No good thing will I withhold from him who walks uprightly (Psalm 84:11). I will give to him good measure, heaped up, shaken together, and running over. I will make him a fruitful branch and a tree whose branches hang over the wall. His abundance cannot be contained. He is not only full but filling others. In drought he shall be fed, and in famine he shall not be hungry. He shall walk in dry places and be refreshed, yea, in stony places and be sustained.

I will love the man who seeks Me, and I will be to him a never ending stream of abundance and he shall never say to another, "Give," but to many shall he say, "Receive."

PSALM 78:15

REMOVE *the* BARRIERS

My children, over many barriers I call to you. Man has erected walls that separate between brothers, but you, My people, have allowed many walls to separate yourselves from the full revelation of My glory.

I do not withhold Myself by choice, but you prevent Me from fellowshipping with you. Curtains of doubt, fear, timidity, unrepentance, and many others hide My face from you so that you cannot know Me.

I plead with you, yes, I cry out to you that before it is too late you will turn to Me with no devices of self-defense, and then can I open My heart to you and pour out My blessings.

ROMANS 10:21

CONTINUAL PRAISE

You will find courage in the hour of calamity if you have disciplined your spirit to rest always in the Lord and to praise continually regardless of circumstances. Any lesser plane of thinking is not only disquieting to the soul but will also open the door to a host of sins. Anger, resentment, petulance, bitterness—none of which can live in an atmosphere of praise—will thrive if the eyes of the soul are diverted to the natural situation and are not fixed on Christ. He deliberately rewards them that adore Him with mercies denied the self-concerned.

Relinquishment of burdens and fears begins where adoration and worship of God becomes the occupation of the soul.

1 THESSALONIANS 5:18

THE POWER *of* HOLINESS

The devil, My child, does not seek to destroy the vile man so much as the holy one. The reprobate is not threatening the kingdom of darkness, he is part of it. All hell trembles when God's prophet takes command in the Name of Jesus over evil powers. This is the man who is hated by the adversary. This is he whom the devil desires to silence. His righteousness has made him a target for the fiery darts of the wicked one. But, lo, I say to you, though all hell should rise against him, I will give My servant power to stand, and he shall know in the very midst of the onslaught that his own soul is being preserved by the very power of holiness within him, which is My own Spirit, and which is the true objective of the enemy.

For truly this power of holiness, this devastating force with which he is able to move against evil and by which he is given power to deliver other men from satanic attack, is My own Holy Spirit dwelling in his temple, giving to him a ministry of deliverance, and resisting evil forces which rise against his own soul.

Is it not written that "He who is with you is GREATER than he who is in the world"? The more My Holy Spirit reigns within, the more intensified becomes the conflict. Fear nothing except the treachery of your own heart that would tell you that in your own strength you can be victorious. The Lord Jesus Christ, through the indwelling presence of His Holy Spirit, HE ALONE is able to keep you from falling and present you blameless before the presence of His glory with exceeding joy.

JUDE 24

THE SECRET PLACE

Many struggles lie in your path, My child, and many dangerous places. You will spare your soul by refusing to countenance evil, and by constantly being reminded that there is a power always working for your protection.

There is always a place of freedom from all evil. It is the abiding in the Secret Place. It is the Ninety-first Psalm. It is what the Psalmist was sharing of his own discovery. In moments of calamity and great danger, he knew a place of perfect peace and complete safety: It was in the heart of God and in his own inner identification with the infinite spirit of holiness.

Holiness brings its own protection. The man who walks in holiness is surrounded by the light and presence of God. In God's light and presence is the power to dispel all forces of darkness and evil regardless of the form they take.

PSALM 91:9-10

FLEE COMPROMISE

O My people, the hour is late and the time for sleeping is past. Gird on the armor of truth and righteousness, and know that the battle is in full array.

Not by might nor by power, but by My Spirit shall you be victorious, so do not seek to outwit the enemy by fleshly strategy. Only as you go *in the strength of the Lord* shall you stand.

Flee compromise, for it leads always to defeat. The shed blood of Christ is your only protection. When you go into battle, go in My Name, and know that you go against an already defeated foe.

Claim the victory, and know that it is yours as you act in faith, not doubting, not retreating, and not arbitrating with the enemy.

ROMANS 8:37

FAMILY *of the* FIRSTBORN

Be alert, for time is moving swiftly. No eye shall discern the preparation for My coming except the eye that is single. Many shall see the signs in the earth of end-time conditions, for these are apparent to all, but I would have My children sensitive in the Spirit, living in the Spirit, discerning in the Spirit. So shall they know the *ministry of preparation* moving throughout the earth at this crucial hour to perfect and make ready a body of people, yes, the FAMILY OF THE FIRSTBORN who shall rejoice and enter into the inheritance of the children of light.

The world's darkness is deceptive, because the natural eye beholds and asks, "Where are the righteous, and where are they who follow the Lamb?" The eye of the Spirit looks abroad and sees the lights of the saints of God as one beholds stars shining in a night sky above a globe enshrouded by storm clouds.

Know that My grace and mercy are intensified, not *in spite of*, but *because of* the tensions of the end-time. Know that My love is moving in surrendered hearts and producing a quality of dedication, zeal, and awareness unsurpassed in the spiritual heroes of the past.

Lift up your heads: Lift up your hearts. Let your faith and courage be reinforced. For in the Spirit you shall listen and hear the sound of a great army readying for battle, and there shall be the sound of going in the tops of the mulberry trees,* and they who have been enlisted by the Spirit shall go forth conquering and to conquer.

*1 CHRONICLES 14:15

THE PATH *of* RIGHTEOUSNESS

(LUKE 1:74–75)

Do not expose your soul to darkness. When you choose the company of those who are not living and walking in the Spirit, you bring to bear upon your soul many evil forces. You may not be aware of this because it is an action not seen by the natural eye. If you were seeing in the Spirit, it would be very real to you, and you would flee from the influence as one runs from a devouring fire or a venomous snake.

Many of the tortures your soul has endured have sprung from your deliberate association with those who walk in spiritual darkness. They may be attractive to the eye as was the fruit which tempted Eve, but if you were living in prayer you would be given the discernment to know the danger of compromise with unyielded vessels. Discernment, My child, is not the spirit of *condemnation.* You are not given the right to condemn, but you SHALL be given the eyes of the Spirit to alert you to danger. I have given something similar to this even to the animals who are very keen to sense the approach of an enemy. Would I do less for you, to protect your soul from the destroyer? No, My child, I will surely give you what is needed for your preservation if you confess your need of My help in this respect and if you *desire* to escape and are willing to choose to walk in a place of higher communion with Me.

Be alert, and do not let man turn you aside. Know that to be kind to your own soul is more important than to try to be kind to those who are rejecting and denying Me, even though it is your desire to influence them for good. Some, the Bible says, should be *"save[d] with fear, pulling them out of the fire; hating even the garment spotted by the flesh"* (Jude 23).

There are ways to witness without compromising, but there is no way to compromise and at the same time effectively witness. *"Come out from among them, and be ye separate,"* says the Word (2 Corinthians 6:17). This command has not been altered. Come out! Those who seek the light will be drawn out into the light. Those who remain in the darkness, it is written, do so because they PREFER the darkness to the light; and to go back into darkness yourself, hoping to save them, will result in giving the evil one the opportunity to assail your own soul.

"Be ye holy for I am holy" (1 Peter 1:15–16). You can never do this while associating with evil, regardless of seemingly noble intentions. Withdraw your foot from the place of sin and compromise, even if it means that you must walk alone in the paths of righteousness. I never promised you the companionship of *others,* but I have promised to walk with you *Myself,* and this blessing you most certainly forfeit when you company with those who are being influenced by all sorts of spirits of evil.

You cannot have both—light and darkness, for what fellowship has Christ with Belial (2 Corinthians 6:14–18)? How shall you walk with Me unless you walk upon the Highroad? I will bless and strengthen you, and your heart shall be light and your spirit shall be ministered unto by My presence.

Angels guard you when you walk with Me. What better way could you choose?

PSALM 140

RECOGNIZE ME *as* YOUR SOURCE

A man may have understanding without holiness, but none can have holiness without understanding. True understanding of God comes only after the heart has ceased to reach to human beings as a source of life and help. As you recognize Me as your source, you immediately become a channel and dispenser of life and need to look to no other. Man can never fail you when you are looking to Me. Man fails you when you look to man.

Be as the bird who trusts his body to the air. Soar in faith on the wings of the Spirit. My Spirit is everywhere—in you, and about you. Discern My presence. Absorb Me as a sponge absorbs water. I am pouring out upon you. Let your heart respond to My love. Receive Me as a cup receives wine. I am your joy and blessing. I am your life and strength.

Angels listen for your songs, for your voice rises to the very gates of heaven when you praise Me.

PRAISE, My child, and I will revive your spirit and renew your faith.

PSALM 138:1–8

INNER CALM

Let nothing disturb your quietness of spirit, for from the place of inner calm you draw courage to move forward through all obstacles. I am never the source of turbulence. Man may REACT with turbulence when I am dealing with his soul, but whenever he does so, it is because his will is in rebellion and he has stiffened his neck. My disciplines are received with peace in the heart that is submissive to My will.

Never console the one who pines under My chastening rod lest you hinder the work of grace I am effecting in his heart and become an obstacle to his spiritual growth.

JOB 22:21

BE DEAF *to the* CRY *of the* CROWD

But he passing through the midst of them went his way.

LUKE 4:30

Ah, My child, this is the secret! Always there will be those who are crowding the way. They will seem to cover the path. If you give power to their words and actions, they will encompass you and prevent your moving ahead. You will feel helpless and confused by their numbers and their noise. GO YOUR WAY.

The moment you set your spiritual eye upon the goal I have given you, the bondage of people is broken. You will be able, as Jesus was, to pass through the midst of them and be freed to be about your Father's business. Do not allow yourself to be trapped by the multitude. Your own higher vision will free you, and there is a path in the Spirit, if you walk in it, where there is free motion. No soul can hinder another soul in this realm. You move in it whenever you move in My will.

If the multitude is pressing in, come up into the Spirit. I will allow nothing to hinder if you are moving in the Spirit. It is when you are in the flesh that you encounter inter-personal confusion. It will trap not only your body but your soul and spirit. I will always free you in the instant that you recapture your vision. You know My demands upon you. Keep responding to *My* demands.

Be deaf to the cry of the crowd.

EPHESIANS 2:1–6

ENDURANCE

My child, do not flinch under My disciplines. I never send more than you can endure, but often I know that is more than you think. Can you accept the cup of suffering as readily as you embrace joy? You can do so in greater degrees as your trust in Me increases. If you know I only send what is for your good, you will see all things good and will know it passes through My love as it comes to you.

My love never fails, even when it brings you pain. My love endures all things (1 Corinthians 13:7) and it will teach you to do likewise. It is in the patient endurance of affliction that the soul is seasoned with grace. It is a barren life that holds only happiness. Saints are not nurtured by levity. Hope does not spring from good fortune.

Hold sacred *every experience.*

ROMANS 5:3–5

SPEAK *the* WORD *of* FAITH

Learn to SPEAK the word of faith and the word of knowledge as I put it in your mouth. Doors will be opened in this simple, God-ordained fashion, and entrance given to hearts that would otherwise have remained closed to the gospel. Once the door is open, you may plant the seed of faith within this newly opened heart, and it will spring forth into eternal life.

Go not to those who are dull of hearing, for I say to you,

their deafness will only increase. Go to the tender. Go to the needy. Go to the brokenhearted and the suffering. I shall minister in love and compassion, and I shall use you as My mouthpiece. You shall do valiantly because the Lord is your strength. You shall go swiftly, for time is running out. You shall go unhindered because I will remove every weight.

LUKE 10:2

SPIRITUAL VICTORY

In tenderness Thou hast brought me to this place, and surely in gentleness Thou wilt minister to my needs. I shall not be disheartened if I may but look upon Thy face. I may not receive a speedy answer to my prayer, but while the light is withheld, I shall trust Thee in the darkness.

My child, spiritual victory is a state of being, not the result of some fortuitous situation; therefore it can be experienced at any time or in any place.

There are many pitfalls in the journey of the soul. It is not given you to know in advance all the hazards, but it is My intention to show you clearly where to set your foot as you take each step.

Guidance and understanding would be relatively simple if all My children understood that I guard their STEPS. Too many habitually pray to have clear sight for *tomorrow,* when they should be praying for light and direction for *TODAY.* All tomorrows rest on today. Tomorrow I keep for you: TODAY I give to you.

What you do with today determines what I will be enabled to give you tomorrow.

"The steps of a good man are ordered by the LORD" (Psalm 37:23).

31

AN OPEN VESSEL

Be about My business. Hold back nothing from Me. The fulness of My blessing moves through the sensitivity of your soul. The callous block Me out. It is not that I do not care for them, but it is that I find no response.

Give Me an open vessel into which I may pour My Spirit. Though it be of clay, it shall overflow with glory.

ROMANS 15:13

THE FATHER'S HOUSE

In My Father's house are many mansions, and there is a place for you, My child. Look not for a place in the world. Your place is in the Father's house. Your soul can rest even now only in the place I provide.

Your restlessness is due to your involvement in things other than My ordained will for you. You have come to a place where you cannot fulfill My purposes for you without singleness of mind. Learn to confine yourself to the Father's house and live within His limitations. It is confining because it excludes the world with its demands and intrusions. You are not of the world, even as I was not of the world. All that is of the world passes away, with its desires. The spirit is nourished only by the eternal, and in prayer the soul breathes the atmosphere of heaven.

Longings are silenced and desires transformed. Christ is sovereign, and the heart rejoices that it is so.

PSALM 27:4

CONSTANCY

My child, My love, My little one, do not let your heart be discouraged. I am nearer you than ever in the past. I have brought you up to a place of constancy, and I will hold you firm regardless of what you are feeling.

You do not need always to see My face to know I am near. You may touch My hand by faith in moments when it is too dark to see *anything*. Never let darkness frighten you. My Spirit is everywhere. . .even in the darkness. You associate Me with joy and light, so that where there is sorrow or pain you question My nearness, and when you do this, you open a door to fear.

PSALM 139:12

THE ECHO *of* MY VOICE

O My child, the cry of your soul is the echo of My voice calling you to repentance. Your love for Me will place you under My chastening rod, for as long as you love Me, you will seek My face even when you anticipate My reproach. The hand of punishment that restores to fellowship is kinder than the hand of sympathy of the one who would palliate your conscience in an evil action.

Much evil is countenanced even among those who profess My Name, and you will be often deceived if you judge what is right or wrong by the opinions of men. My Spirit searches the deep things of the heart. I not only taste the fruit; I test the soundness of the tree. I do not look at the leaves but examine the roots. I behold not the shape of the tree but test the heart.

So it is with you. What man accepts as good is often evil in My sight because My Spirit always probes the heart. Whenever you come to Me in repentance, it is this that I show you. . .not the outward display of leaves, but the rottenness in the core.

Let Me deal with any unsoundness in your spirit, and I will spare you the humiliation of open shame. Inner conviction comes through My Word, and this is your only sure way of finding peace in My presence.

Do not act and then seek My approval, but seek first My face, and then whatever I lead you to do will be an expression of your love for Me and will be pure in My sight because it has issued out of the wellspring of My love. Anything else is false and will wither and die.

MATTHEW 23:25-28

THE DISCIPLINES *of* FREEDOM

O My people, I bring you out of bondage as rapidly as you are able to cope with freedom. I have led you by the way of the wilderness because in the discipline of lack coupled with liberty, the soul learns true obedience to God and is strengthened in faith.

The newly freed man, while rejoicing in his liberty, knows not how to use it wisely. The chains have fallen from his feet, but his soul is still in fetters. Moses had eighty years of freedom before he led the children of Israel out of the bondage of Egypt. A slave could not have led them out. Only a free man could lead them out, for bondage generates dependence and destroys initiative and a sudden flight from Egypt does not immediately restore these powers. Slavery destroys the individual sense of responsibility. It denies man his personal dignity and forces him to be subject to man rather than to God. In all these areas there must be restoration when freedom is effected.

Thus I say unto you, My children, hold fast in the liberty wherein I have set you free and allow not man to bring you back into subjection. The children of Israel through many hard lessons learned to accept the leadership of Moses, but this was *obedience*, not BONDAGE. They were taught to respect God-ordained authority, but they were severely punished when they expressed a desire to return to the slavery of Egypt for the comfort of the flesh and satisfaction of carnal appetites. Many times they would gladly have exchanged the disciplines of freedom for the ease of slavery, for slavery imposes no responsibility for individual action. Personal response to the challenge of a higher call is impossible to the slave, so the soul is bound as well as the body.

The tyranny of Egypt and the soul-destroying influences of bondage to man are more than history: They are the present challenge of My people today as they are freed from bondage to man and loosed in the Spirit. You are freed, My people, not to use your liberty as an opportunity to express self-will, but you are freed to learn the holy discipline of the Spirit and to become a true bond slave of Jesus Christ, honoring Him in the liberty He provides. . .the liberty to choose to serve and follow the only One who is truly free.

All sin is binding. In Christ is freedom, because in Him is holiness. Your constant desire for purity is your safeguard against the desire to return to the fleshpots and the slavery of Egypt, which is always a symbol of the world. The world with its desires passes away, but he who chooses to do the will of God will live forever.

To bemoan the tasteless bread of divine discipline and harbor a hidden hunger for the exotic diet of the world as the children of Israel loathed the manna is to resist the liberating power of the Holy Spirit at work in your own soul. Every challenge and every choice moves you either backward to the bondage of Egypt or forward to the full blessing of the promised land.

An entire generation perished in the wilderness because of indecision, for though they were bodily freed, they never wakened to their spiritual liberty, of whom it is written that they grieved the Spirit of God for forty years and died in the wilderness, never having received the promise (Hebrews 3:15–19).

Bringing you out, My children, is only the beginning. I am bringing sons to glory, and I say unto you, I am preparing a people who SHALL GO IN. They SHALL POSSESS THE LAND. They SHALL BE STRONG IN THE LORD, and they shall fulfill My purposes (Joshua 1).

Think not that all bondage comes upon you by the actions of other men. True liberation of your own spirit is yours as you are freed from enslavement to your own will and the selfish demands of your own flesh. For there is an inner world of spiritual combat in every soul where dwell both Egypt and Canaan and a wilderness battleground in between. My eye ever searches this inner man of each of My children to find the secret overcomer.

GALATIANS 5:1

RECOGNITION *and* FOCUS

Recognition, My child, brings Me into focus. It is not so much your actions as your motives which concern Me; for I know that from pure motives spring good works, just as a loving heart spontaneously prompts gentle manners.

Recognition is the sight I give your inner eye to discern distortion of My image in your own character. I do not say in your *brother's*, but in *your own!* I would have your personality patterns display My character, and wherever this fails to be so, there is distortion of the image, and in such state, as others look to you for guidance and inspiration, they do not see a clear image of Me.

2 CORINTHIANS 3:18

CLOSED DOORS

Never lose heart when confronted by disappointment, for if you will take time for recollection, many past experiences will come to mind in which the closed door proved to be a blessing as it left you free to accept a different and greater opportunity.

Remember always that I control all that touches you, and as I move to order your life, I not only open the right doors but close the wrong ones. Whenever a wrong door is closed, it is by My hand as much as when a right one opens. In this way I not only bring you joy but spare you pain. Trust Me.

Never bemoan what seems to have been lost. All things are gathered into My bosom and I return to you only what will bless. As you trust Me when things appear to be going wrong, your anxiety will diminish. Have I not said that nothing shall harm you?

LUKE 10:19

RELATING *to* JOY

In every moment of joy, it is I who am blessing you. Over and over I have come to reveal My love through others and concealed My presence in the fortuitous circumstance. Be not deceived by the appearance. All actions that bear upon your life are second causes. I am the first and only true source of good. You will receive a double portion of joy when you recognize My love coming to you through the kindness of others and when you learn to express your gratitude both to them and to Me.

Much has been written about My will moving through adversity, and from this awareness men draw courage in the hour of loss. I say to you, if you discern My love *in every moment of happiness,* you will multiply a thousandfold your capacity to fully enjoy your blessings.

Man is unable to be happy in his happiness and to rejoice in

38

his joys because he does not relate himself to My love for him and therefore blocks his own receptivity. He cannot abandon himself to joy because of memories of past pain and fear of future loss. He is robbed by the past and frightened by the future. He cannot free himself of either his remembered disappointments or his anticipated losses.

When rightly related to Me, joys are stabilized by the constancy of My love. The happiness thereby identified with Me as its source ceases to be destroyed by insecurity. When you are able to receive and fully accept all good in this way, you honor Me as truly as when you are patient in adversity.

Open your heart wide to life. The good I will bless yet more, and the rest I will transform. Restraint binds, and pessimism poisons even that which would otherwise be sweet.

PSALM 68:19

MY WORDS CANNOT WAIT

The hour is late, and the time for ministering is limited. Delay not, but hasten to finish the work. I have other work for you, and it waits only the completion of the present task. Do that which is nearest at hand. I shall open a way for its fulfillment, so you need not hold back, wondering how the provisions will be supplied. Lacked you ever in the past? Have you not acted in each case with faith in Me as your only hope? Yes, My child, I say to you, walk on. There are no limits to the promises of your God.

My words cannot wait; but you have held them as though you thought the future would wait. Up! Delay no more. Obey

Me, and do so quickly. There is a door open that may soon be shut. There are hearts ready that will be turned in discouragement to error but for your words. Send forth the message and trust Me with its end. I hold all things in My power, and I shall direct its goings. Hold not back the message from any seeking soul. Do not analyze the situation nor seek to protect yourself from misunderstanding nor My words from rejection.

Lo, the Spirit accompanies the word, and you may know and be confident that My Spirit anointing the page will bring light and revelation and the confession that God has truly spoken. Yield and labor. I will add the blessing and the reward. I have called you by name. I have given you My words, and I will not have them set aside either by you or by others.

Renew your faith. Look directly to Me. I will empower and I will make all things possible as you move in obedience.

PHILIPPIANS 1:6

FOREWARNED *and* FOREARMED

Never waver once you have clear guidance. If you set out to do what I have bidden and sudden fear grips your heart, know that it is a device of the enemy. I am not the author of fear but of courage and a settled mind.

Confusion is the dust raised by the feet of the devil, calculated to cloud your vision and blind your eyes to the good I have placed directly in your path, and which you will surely find if you continue to act in faith.

To be forewarned of the treachery of Satan is to be fore-armed to deal with it swiftly and effectively. The soldier who is decorated for bravery is the one who has faced a crisis and grappled with the forces of death. Even so, to win the prize of the high calling in Christ Jesus requires a willingness to endure the onslaughts of the enemy and lay down life itself, if need be, that God's will may be sovereign.

PHILIPPIANS 3:12-14

DELIGHT *in* ME

Bear patiently the trials of each day. They would seem insignificant if you were more deeply conscious of My presence. When you are near Me, you have peace and joy and rest of soul: Prayer is natural and praise a delight. When your eyes are upon Me, you are never in consternation about circumstances. Loving Me with fervor gives grace to forgive and love others.

Delight yourself in Me. I will turn your sighs to shouts and your defeats to victories.

PSALM 37:4-5

PROTECTION *from* EVIL

My kingdom is not of this world. In multiplicity of duties you may lose sight of Me momentarily, but even in the most pressing circumstances you will discover My presence with you if you pause to worship Me silently in your heart. Never fear that activity will crowd Me out. I will be very real to you at all times if you do not let the confusion that is around you in the world invade your inner sanctuary.

Did I not promise to put a garrison around your heart (Philippians 4:7)? Why do you think I put it there if not to shut out the world with all its soul-destroying influences? I do not shut out the things that will bless you, the pure and beautiful, but as you trust Me to protect you from evil, this garrison becomes as a screen that lets in whatever will bless and uplift you and shuts out that which would destroy.

All spiritual action operates as you believe and trust. This protecting power is no exception. I shield your soul from destructive influences to the degree that you believe that I can and will, yes, as you *accept* it, and even more, as you DESIRE it to be so.

He who seeks evil will surely find it, but he who longs after purity will be given divine help, and My Spirit within you will stand against that which would otherwise overpower you.

PSALM 91:1

A YIELDED SPIRIT

The lesson of obedience is still of first importance. Unless you move in obedience, all your other actions and your knowledge will be misdirected and unfruitful. Know My will, and do it. But, you say, How can I know God's will? I have revealed it to you, My child, and I am constantly seeking to guide you in myriad ways. Your self-will blots out My divine directives.

Before the sound of My voice registers on your consciousness, you drown it out with the objections of an unyielded spirit. You will never move freely in My highest purpose unless you constantly offer up to Me a yielded, broken, self-renouncing vessel.

I do not recognize your profession of holy intentions. If your intentions were truly sincere, they would move you out of conviction and into action. You would minister with power if you truly listened for My words and if you were even partially obedient.

PROVERBS 29:1

AN UNCOMPLAINING HEART

Be patient while I deal with you in the areas of your own inner needs. Bear joyfully My rod of correction. Know that while I minister to you, you are being prepared to minister to others. Make no mistake, there cannot be one without the other. Your attitudes need the disciplining of the Holy Spirit.

Rest in Me in the quiet place and give Me an uncomplaining heart. I will fill it with My grace. When I see that you are ready to do it, I will make My will inescapable.

JOB 5:17-18

THE SUN IS ALWAYS SHINING

There is never a moment when I am absent from the scene of your life. Your feeling of separation does not make it so. It is like the sunshine. Clouds enshroud the earth and you say the sun is not shining. This is not true. The sun is *always* shining. The truth is that because it is a cloudy day, you cannot *see* the sun shining. Even so, My grace is always pouring down upon you, and in moments when your own spirit may not discern it, My love is nonetheless constant and real.

Your joy may be restored at any moment as you brush aside the clouds of earth by recapturing the strength of the times when you have felt the warmth of the sunshine, yes, even been blinded by the power of its rays.

PSALM 136

GRIEF

Behold, there is a river of divine grace flowing beneath all your need. Under your deepest sorrow move My compassion and My love. In a very real sense, you fathom the depth of My own heart only to the extent that your heart is broken and your inmost consciousness torn asunder by the pain of grief.

All things to grow require a proper climate. Love, if it is to be given, must also be received. You are never so ready to accept My love as when you are experiencing anguish.

Never look upon trials and testings and disciplines as being damaging. Whatever hurt they seem to bring is outweighed by the blessing which follows.

2 CORINTHIANS 4:17

COUNT IT ALL JOY

Count it all joy, my brethren,
when you meet various trials,
for you know that the testing of your faith
produces steadfastness.

JAMES 1:2–3 RSV

Count it all joy when you face disappointment,
Count it all joy when temptations assail;
Count it all joy when affliction o'ertakes thee,
Count it all joy, for thy God will not fail.

He will sustain in the moment of weakness,
Faith will increase in the place of despair;
Jesus will comfort the heart that is breaking,
Count it all joy, He is hearing your prayer.

He is not willing that any should perish,
He will be present all foes to destroy.
He'll stand between you and all of your sickness;
Praise Him, and love Him, and *count it all joy!*

F J R

WITHDRAW THY FOOT

Robbed of privacy, friendship is destroyed. Invade not the privacy of another life, nor probe where discretion has closed the door. There is a degree of reserve to which each soul has birthright, and which if relinquished to the curiosity of the impudent leaves him stripped of the riches of his soul and robbed of his self-respect, even though that which is thereby discovered be his purest treasure.

Surmise not that secrecy concealeth evil. Grant the soul peace, both your own and others, by cultivating so firm a confidence in the integrity of your friend as to know that were that confidence betrayed, you were yourself no longer worthy to call yourself his friend.

Beat not upon the closed door, nor contrive to be admitted where no invitation has been given.

The poor man, having no riches, has also no vault.

The riches of friendship are placed in the hands of those who prove themselves trustworthy. The ignorant will rob a nest of its eggs. The wise wait patiently for the sound of baby birds. He who steals the eggs deprives himself of this pleasure.

Better to be in the dark than to take by force or subtlety another's lamp. Without the oil to sustain it, the comfort it may bring will be short lived.

Any comfort forcibly extracted from another soul will turn to ashes in the hand. Curiosity does not befit the saint, and he will neither probe the soul of another nor feel deprived of information not yet given.

PROVERBS 26:20

WISDOM, *a* GIFT

Much false doctrine has been generated out of man's fleshly desire to possess knowledge not yet revealed. In his impertinence, he has resented even the silence of God and expressed his intolerance of this silence by fabricating ideas of his own to fill the vacuum of ignorance.

O foolish creature! To have the mind filled with information is a questionable blessing. Knowledge and wisdom are a gift from God. Information wrongly acquired or inaccurately interpreted becomes a curse rather than a blessing. Be content to know only what is freely revealed by either God or man, and be not a scavenger of information. Let your lips be taught to share truth and disdain idle words, evil surmising, and gossip.

PROVERBS 20:19

BROKENNESS

Brokenness comes only by the hand of the Holy Spirit upon the human heart. The storms of life may make shipwreck of a soul, but this may be purely destructive. The brokenness of spirit wrought by the hand of God becomes a *constructive* work. It is the godly sorrow unto repentance that brings Life.

The soul abounds in grace when prayer is its breath, and true prayer is born out of brokenness. This brokenness is a contrition for sins, tenderness of feeling, and gratitude for grace. Yes, My child, and if you will let it work in your heart, it will

47

surely draw you closer and closer to Me; but if you harden your heart and refuse to allow Me to deal with you in this way, you will turn one day to seek Me and will not find Me.

2 CORINTHIANS 7:10

A DEVOURING FIRE

When the enemy shall come in like a flood,
the Spirit of the Lord shall lift up a standard against him.

ISAIAH 59:19

Be prepared, O My people, and know that darkness is ever moving against My Church. It moves against you as a believer, but I have promised to deliver, and he who walks in prayer shields his soul from the enemy.

Hold forth the word of truth, both receiving it and giving it, for it is a devouring fire as it goes forth against evil. Lo, it is written, that when I come, I shall destroy the wicked with the words of My mouth (Revelation 19:15, Hebrews 4:12). You shall be able to scatter much darkness and combat the powers of evil as you speak My Word in faith.

DEVOTION *and* WARFARE

Presume not to labor to build with the right hand without holding the sword in the left (Nehemiah 4:18). It is vigilance

COMBINED with prayer that spells victory. Devotion must be coupled with warfare to be fruitful. Holy ecstasy must be mixed with holy boldness, and love must be blended with courage. Only to pray is not enough. Prayer must rise from the battlefield of spiritual conquest.

SOUND *the* TRUMPET

Be alert. Be vigilant. Sound the trumpet in Zion, the alarm from My holy mountain. Challenge My people that they be not overtaken by the enemy because they have a false sense of security. By My Spirit you shall overcome, and by My Word you shall prevail.

Gird on the armor of My holiness, and speak the word of faith. Fear not the enemy; for he has already been stripped of his power, and victory is yours as you stand in the strength of the Lord. Surely I will send My delivering angel to stand beside you, and you shall not turn back, neither give in to weariness, for the Lord your God, He is your strength, and in His hand is the reward.

THE BENT *of the* SOUL

In every place you go, there am I to meet you. Move in the joy of knowing I am in the midst.

I am in the midst of sorrow and joy alike. I am in business

as surely as I am in the sanctuary of worship. In fact, the former becomes the proving ground of the latter. Be content in ALL places and be at ease in your spirit. You know the truth of My omnipresence, but you need to experience it more deeply. You must learn it *quickly* because you are an example to others.

It is in testings that you are made strong. Do not run from them in search of Me. I have set up circumstances and have set you in the midst of them. It is the work of the devil to pull down. If he cannot prevent you from finding a platform for action, he will try to make you think some other kind of ministry would be more blessed. It is your own inner consecration that hallows the outer action. Two may do what appears to be the same work. To one it is holy and to the other it is carnal. The difference is in the bent of the soul. . .whether it be for the glory of God or for self-aggrandizement. I breathe My very life into that which is offered to Me as a sacrifice of love.

Offer daily to Me ALL I have entrusted to you, and you will discover an ever-increasing sense of spiritual harmony.

COLOSSIANS 3:17

FAITH RELEASED

Lean hard on Me, My child, and I will be your peace. Storm shall not disquiet the trusting heart, but songs of praise and victory shall spring from the place of testing, and mercy shall prevail where faith is released, in spite of every contrary wind.

No harm can come to the one who looks to Me as his protection, but he who endeavors to protect himself shall be exposed to the destructive forces he seeks to escape.

He shall not know peace who runs after the rewards of the world.

MATTHEW 16:25

BLESSINGS *of the* OBEDIENT

Happy is the man who follows in the footsteps of his Lord. He shall not serve strange masters neither walk in dark places. The Lord shall be his strength and wisdom, and his heart shall rejoice in the confidence of knowing: God is my judge; He is also my Saviour. He shall be upon my right hand, standing beside me, and I shall not fall into the snare of discouragement.

Surely the days shall bring this man joy and happiness, and life shall open to him her treasures. He shall be courageous. He shall do exploits. He shall rejoice that in the day of battle he finds power to stand. His heart shall be at peace because his mind is stayed on God.

Though others be distracted, his eyes are fixed on Jesus, and no turmoil disturbs his inner calm. This peace the world can never give, but it is the possession of the obedient man, because he has made the Most High, even the Everlasting Father, his habitation. He shall not taste defeat!

PSALM 1

PRAYER, *a* MEANS *of* GROWTH

My children, I hear your prayers before they are voiced, but I listen still for your cry because I delight that you come to Me with your needs. It is in the contact of loving hearts, as one responds to the other's plea, that fellowship is established. I could arrange to have all your requirements supplied in such a way that no requests would be necessary, but you would be unmindful of the source of your good.

When you are forced to beg Me for your needs, you then accept My supply with a grateful spirit. This all contributes to the progress of your soul in faith and grace. The experience of prayer answered is of only incidental importance in comparison to your growth in grace and spiritual maturity.

Your love for Me also deepens as you pray and receive an answer, for each answer is evidence of My concern for you and desire to bless. The more you pray, the more My love is revealed to you; thus your faith is growing strong by reason of exercise, but also your heart is being melted by My love for you and your response.

MATTHEW 6:6

THE SHADOW *of* MY HAND

Peace, My child, is the shadow of My hand. When your soul is at rest, it is because you are consciously aware of My presence. You do not need to seek peace. As you realize My nearness, you will discover that I am there, in the center of your worship; for to seek Me is to desire to worship Me. Finding Me, you have no need to seek peace, for *I Myself am your peace.*

JOHN 14:27

MERCY

Mercy is the extension of My grace. Whenever you show mercy to another, you express My love. I rejoice in forgiveness. I do not give grudgingly. You have been told to give cheerfully of your substance; now I say unto you, do the same in the Spirit. When you are called upon to be tolerant—to forgive—do not question and do not delay, lest you damage another soul, and your own no less.

Deal justly, but in patience and understanding, and add not evil upon evil. As I have given to you, so likewise do you to others, otherwise you violate My mercy as it would flow through you.

PSALM 103:8–18; LUKE 6:35–38

A COVERT *in the* STORM

Be at peace, My little one, for in Me there is a covert in the storm. My love remains changeless whatever winds may blow. My grace will sustain you however deep may be the night, however fierce may be the test.

Nothing harms the trusting soul though calamity be his

companion. In affliction there shall be comfort, for he who abides in Me shall not know desolation. I protect, I provide, I enrich. None shall say in My presence, "I am poor," for he who loves Me is supremely blessed; My grace is his strength, and I am his salvation.

The lowly shall know Me and shall rejoice in My Name. I will honor him who honors Me and will lift up the one who humbles himself at My feet.

1 PETER 5:5–7

VICTORY *in* ADVERSITY

Whenever you experience pain, know that I am knocking at the door of your heart.

Nothing should be of any real concern to you except your relationship to Me and a right attitude toward others. Life brings unpleasant circumstances, but I say unto you, I am in the midst, causing all experiences, both pleasant and otherwise, to harmonize for your blessing and growth.

I do not shield you from hardship. I give you victory while in the throes of adversity.

ROMANS 8:28

MY WORD, YOUR STAFF

Be vigilant, for the enemy has many wiles. You are no match for his subtlety. He torments the people of God with evil suggestions. You are never immune to the infectious germs of sin. Your soul needs a daily transfusion of the blood of Jesus to build resistance. Only His life pulsating through your spiritual veins can keep you strong and holy. Be constantly mindful that Christ alone is your source of victory. The flesh profits nothing.

Your own reasonings are insufficient in the face of satanic strategy. You need the wisdom that comes by My Spirit, and you need the boldness produced by prayer and confidence in My written Word, the Holy Bible. It is your staff. . .that which you may lean upon. Lean heavily, and I will undertake for you.

If you ask My help and give Me a free hand to work in your life, you need never fall into the snare of the enemy.

1 PETER 5:8

ANCHOR YOUR FAITH *in* ME

Sacrifice and deprivation are nothing when they lead to a closer walk with your God. I would bring you into a place of consecration that will make possible a ministry which is beyond your present capacity. I know the way you take, and though it is now veiled to you, I am preparing the details and making ready the very things and the people who will have a part in fulfilling My purposes in your life.

Go not about to inquire of others, for how can they possibly know My plan for you? No, My child, LOOK TO ME ALONE. My love for you is matched with My wisdom, and I am moving in your behalf. Anchor your faith in ME. I ALONE will uphold you and sustain you and supply the needed strength.

As I have told you before, I will not ask more than I give grace to do.

PSALM 138:8

GUARD *the* GARRISON

It is good to solicit the prayers of God's people, but this must never be substituted for personal combat. There is a time to bear one another's burdens, and there is a time for every man to bear his own (Galatians 6:2, 5). Study to know the difference, and do not let the devil gain an advantage over you while you are resting in the hope that the prayers of others will preserve your own soul.

"Be sober, be vigilant," it is written.

Presume not upon another to be vigilant in your behalf. To you is given the sacred charge of guarding your own soul. Negligence is as sinful as self-will.

Confess your laxity, and give heed to the warning. God's help awaits the wakened soul.

1 PETER 5:8

SING *and* BE GLAD

Rejoice, My child, for I have delivered you from the treachery of the enemy. Walk no more in slippery places presuming on

My divine protection and intervention. Know that you can receive from Me the wisdom to AVOID the pits of confusion and make a way for you that is a way of holy action with no compromise and no darkness. You do not have to LOOK for a way. I have CREATED it especially for you.

Seek My face and do My bidding, and follow My direction explicitly and you will find yourself IN My perfect will—not seeking it. It will APPEAR. It will be inescapable. It will be natural and easy. *No man shall be able to hinder or destroy My work.* I will create it in and through you, and you shall know that it has come pure from My hand.

Rejoice! Have no fear concerning ANYTHING, and look at no time to your own ability to produce the results. I do it Myself; for it is My Word, not your word, and I will move heaven and earth if necessary to preserve it.

Be of good cheer. Sing and be glad, for this day is a day of victory and a day of deliverance. This day is a day of joy, yes, to My own heart, for I delight to answer prayer and to make the crooked straight.

I will restore and bless a hundredfold.

PSALM 52:8-9

WARRING *in the* SPIRIT

Out of many varied experiences the soul gains knowledge, and knowledge brings strength and stability. It is vain to battle the spiritual elements with the carnal mind. Only the man who is taught of the Spirit can war in the Spirit. You must war, because there are enemies unseen to the eye of man but constantly besieging the child of God. But he is not left defenseless. Heavenly protection is his as well as offensive weapons. The sword of the Spirit, the blood of the Lamb, and the word of testimony are provided for every saint of God but must be put into action in faith before they can effect a deliverance.

No passive spirit can ever be effective at this point. Aggression is imperative because there is an aggressive enemy to be met and overcome. Jesus on many occasions demonstrated this fact and moved directly into the front line of attack against the devil. You must do the same.

REVELATION 12:11

GOOD *and* EVIL

Every foot of ground where you tread, that will I give you. Walk in faith, and I will reward you with an abundance of fruit.

It is not in the heart of a man to discern his own way. Much that is evil man calls good, and much that is good men curse because a man will bless what he enjoys and condemn what gives him displeasure.

I say unto you, My hand does not always deal joy. Joy may come in the end, but the initial action may bring pain. Fear not. I am not only wise but kind, and today's grief may become the channel for tomorrow's blessing.

PHILIPPIANS 4:11–12

PRESS ON

O My child, you have crossed a bridge. Reach not back.
Move on ahead and press into the fulness of all I have prepared
for you. It is the blossoming of that which long ago was planted
and for many years has been nurtured. It is waiting for you to step
forward and receive. Do not tarry, and do not question, neither
allow doubts to enter your mind. Your heart may cry out and
rebel, but if you will turn to Me in those moments, I will give you
My peace. I send you no place except as I have gone before.

PHILIPPIANS 3:14

LIBERTY

All [his] works are truth, and his ways judgment;
and those that walk in pride he is able to abase.

DANIEL 4:37

Stand fast in the liberty wherein I have made you free and
allow no man to move you into a position of compromise. I have
loosed you for reasons not yet revealed to you. There will come a
time when you will understand more fully why I have done so.
Be diligent to make the most of the opportunities thus afforded
you, and do not miss any.

You will never discover what I have planned for you if in
your zeal you run ahead and become again entangled. I free you,

and I want to keep you free. Why do you look to others for help when I am already at work moving mountains, opening doors, and touching hearts on your behalf?

I am penetrating the darkness with My light. Claim the victory. I will bring it to pass. I search all hearts, and I will bring conviction upon the wrongdoer and cause righteousness to displace injustice. I will not suffer My light to be extinguished nor My Word to be set at naught.

Be at peace.

THE SPIRITUAL REALM

Do not be concerned about failing *people*. Your only true concern should be that you not fail *ME*. I am making last-minute preparations for My soon-coming. The table is already spread for the marriage supper of the Lamb. Do not frustrate My plans for you by pursuing your own. When your schedule is arranged in advance, there is no room in your life for Me to guide you into My highest and best. It is a contrivance of the enemy working through seemingly natural circumstances to hold you captive to a material world.

I want you walking and expressing in the *spiritual* realm. For this purpose have I painstakingly prepared your soul. Cast aside your carnal reasonings. Cast aside even your consideration for people and the threat of disappointing them. Would you rather that I be disappointed, in preference to others? Furthermore, this anxiety about disappointing others is not based on fact, but on supposition. Can you not *trust* Me? Would I fail anyone? Shall I not move to protect and provide for those you commit into My hand for My care during your days of solitude? They will also come to this place eventually, and they will at that point praise God if at this time you are obedient by becoming an example through your own obedience.

MATTHEW 11:28-29

QUIETNESS

How often have I spoken to you concerning the importance of quietness? You have been obedient partially, but the solitude with which you have surrounded yourself is being invaded and destroyed by the conflicts within your soul.

PSALM 4:4; JOB 22:21

HOLINESS *upon the* HEARTS

I the Lord have tried you. I have placed in your path the open pit. I have given you the freedom to choose either good or evil. . .to obey Me or to walk in your own way. Be not deceived. Though you see no eye, you are being looked upon, and though you seek no voice, I continue to call.

I have entreated in love and chastened you in pity. Turn to

Me, My child. Open your heart to My grace. I will embrace both you and your need, and you shall say, "Surely the Lord has had mercy upon me and has shown me my wound that He might be gracious to me and heal me of all my sicknesses."

For I say unto you, holiness shall be written upon the hearts of My people, and righteousness over their doors. They shall minister in power because they live in obedience, and if any do not desire obedience and discipline, he shall not be My disciple.

EPHESIANS 1:4

PROVISION

My promises wait their fulfillment in the lives of My children. So much I would give. . .so little is received. Why live so beggarly when the riches of heaven are yours for the asking? Having learned to receive from Me, you will find it easy to give to all others, for you shall have no fear of lack, and no need to guard your supply. Having found the *source,* you shall never want.

David's heart was freed to sing "The Lord is my shepherd," having come to know Him as his *provider.* Rejoice, My children, and walk in the freedom of My abundance, looking not to man, but to Me for ALL things.

PHILIPPIANS 4:19

SUSTAINING GRACE

My child, have I ever failed you in the past? Is the present crisis beyond My power to help? You shall experience My sustaining grace as you venture forth in faith. Let nothing stand in the way. Move in confidence. I am your protection as a wall of fire round about.

Let Me carry the weight of the responsibility. You need not rely on your own intelligence. Let My mind be in you, and receive from Me your guidance. It will never be wrong, and the most clever man cannot devise a means to outwit Me. So lean on My arm of infinite support, and your days shall abound with goodness as an orchard abounds with fruit.

I am your all-sufficiency. I am your source of ALL good. I wish to be your center of attention and total satisfaction. Whatever else I give you is a small token blessing in addition. . . a fringe benefit, if you please.

PSALM 27

THE WAYS *of the* SPIRIT

Do not grieve My Spirit and do not quench His power when He is moving in your own or another vessel. My purifying work is being done in the sacred moments when My anointing is resting upon a soul. Be aware that as a witness, you stand on holy ground, and reverence should be your attitude.

Deep within the soul My Spirit is moving deftly to do a

miraculous work. Do not hinder in any way, however small. It is a holy moment, one in which all the world of natural expression is excluded. Only in eternity shall you fully know the depth of this kind of ministry. Waste not time trying to understand.

The ways of the Spirit are a mystery. I reveal to each individual what is necessary for his own soul's progress. Others do not need to know. Like Saul on the road to Damascus, to him were spoken clear words, while others heard only a sound. Even so, I speak clearly to the one who is slain in the Spirit. Others need not know nor question.

ACTS 9:7

CHALLENGE *and* GROWTH

In all the challenges of life, My hand is outstretched to give you courage. No stress need overwhelm if your confidence is in Me. To lean upon the arm of flesh brings certain disaster. You will never experience My protection and supernatural intervention while you are relying on your own resourcefulness. In the impossible situation you may turn the tide the moment your attention is moved away from the chaos and focused on Me.

When the Psalmist penned "From the Lord comes my help," he excluded all other sources. Only full reliance upon Me produces miraculous results. In this hour of intensified satanic activity, miracles are not a dispensable luxury, they are an everyday necessity. Human cleverness is no match for the devil. Intellectual persuasion will not cast out demons; neither can a faith that wavers bring any kind of deliverance. Effective faith is born of total consecration. My Spirit alone can bring forth this kind of dedication and inner strength.

Continual challenges bring constant growth, and when you pray for respite from the conflict, you rob your soul and retard its maturation.

Hold before Me at all times a heart that prefers instruction to comfort. You cannot have both. Self-preservation rejects suffering. Suffering is an instrument of grace as My Spirit moves through the painful circumstance to bring understanding.

MATTHEW 17:21

STEWARDSHIP *of* TIME

Cherish time and hold it sacred, for you will have to give an account for your stewardship in this regard as surely as in the matter of the use of your money.

Not all possess the same amount of wealth, so one may give more than another; but to every man is given the same amount of time, so none can say "I have had less, so therefore I could give less." Your carefulness in stewardship is the one deciding factor as to how much you give Me of your time. You will give to the degree of your dedication, and the more you give, the greater shall be your reward.

Let nothing rob you of precious hours that could be used in devotion or study or in ministry. That which is lost can never be recaptured.

PSALM 90:4–12

Promptness, Your Safeguard

Learn to obey at the earliest possible moment. Promptness is your safeguard against the treachery of the enemy. If he cannot dissuade you from desiring to do My will, he will try to alter it so you will believe you are doing the right thing, but in actuality he has changed it just enough to make it wrong. He started this strategy with Eve in the Garden of Eden, and it is a device he has found so effective he is still using it. It is because of this hazard that you find I so often do not give guidance in advance. I speak to you with specific directions almost simultaneously with the demand for the action. The more promptly you respond, the more completely will you carry out My purposes.

Psalm 119:60

On Not Resisting Evil

My wisdom will come to you, My child, when you become quiet. Anxiety places the soul in stress. Any response to darkness closes the door to revelation. Clear guidance comes when all demands of the ego are silenced. The strivings of your own heart will be as out of harmony with My Spirit as the evil you wish to combat. This is why the Scripture says "Resist not evil." * The thrust is ineffective because the action is negative.

You cannot correct the crooked path of another, but you can let Me show you how to make a straight path of your own. The straight path will lead into light, but the crooked path will gather darkness and end in confusion.

Never *fear* the darkness. . .AVOID it.

I have given you tools with which to build your own structure. Do not use your energy destroying the house of your enemy. If it is an unsound structure, it will eventually fall. You need your full attention to build rightly your own. Most of all, do not entangle the two lest both be destroyed. Whenever you are tempted to strike out, look for the devices of the ego. The Spirit has no need to respond to threats, because its own creative flow is a more powerful action. This can be yours by continual choices and denial of self.

*MATTHEW 5:39

ANXIETY

Over and over I have spoken to you about being anxious. Nothing retards growth more than apprehension. Fear in any form will bind the soul of a man and imprison his spirit in darkness. The free man fears nothing. The bound sit in prison houses, not knowing how they came there nor how to escape.

REVELATION 21:8

REWARDS *of* DEVOTION

As your soul turns to worship, let it be with one supreme desire: to bring Me your love. Eternity will be a time of rejoicing because all will love Me and find expression for their love. This is not a selfish demand on My part. I can ask of you a full portion, yes, unlimited devotion, because I am a giver, not a taker, and you will always find yourself *enriched* beyond your expectations whenever you give yourself to Me in even a very limited way.

I ask you to give only to bless you more.

JOHN 14:21

ANTICIPATION, MEDITATION, PARTICIPATION

The time is short. As you have honored Me with your lips, honor Me now with your ministry. Move on into that place of active participation in My will. Anticipation, meditation, participation: There is a place for each of these as you move from one to the other, and then back through the same cycle again.

Follow the life of Jesus in the Gospels and you will see this pattern repeated time after time. Never get bogged down at any one of these points. Always move on into the next. I will teach you, but you must not hold back. Out in the field and back to the mountain of prayer and communion. Solitude and then service, and vice versa. Neither is complete in itself. Each is enriched by the other. In solitude I minister *to* you, and in service I minister *through* you to others. Both are essential to your growth, and others are robbed of blessing if you hoard the riches of God and fail to share.

LUKE 21:37-38

The Rod *and the* Look

Wait upon Me. Bask in My presence continually. Seek My face and expose your entire being to the full light of My Spirit. HEAR My words as I speak to YOU, and thus can I do My purging, chastening, and purifying work in you without the need of outer disturbance. The rod of punishment is laid upon the young child to correct and discipline him; but between two lovers, this is not the method. I love you, and as you come into a closer relationship with Me and the maturity of the walk of the true Bride, I do not deal with you as with a child, but as a husband who gently remonstrates with his wife, impressing upon her his thoughts and wishes, often with only a look.

But you cannot receive this type of ministry from Me when you walk afar off. And I will still not deal with you as with a child when you are no longer in that stage. This is why some of My choicest saints find themselves in a time of spiritual lapse feeling not the touch of the chastening rod. Just to draw near Me in a time of failure brings to the sensitive, loving spirit deeper suffering than was ever brought to a disobedient child by the chastening rod.

LUKE 22:61-62

A Consuming Desire

If I lay not My hand upon you in punishment, come near. Look into My eyes. Dare to draw close to My heart. You will know surely My desire and purpose for you and shall grieve more that you have displeased Me and caused Me grief than that you may have forfeited some personal gain or blessing. You will not view your spiritual walk as a challenge to be a successful Christian in the eyes of men but will have a consuming desire to please Me and bring only joy to My heart.

GALATIANS 1:10

FOLLY *of* IMMATURITY

It is so simple when you approach Me in proper fashion and do not hinder your spiritual progress by regression to a parent-child position in your attitude. I know full well when you are no longer properly in that stage, and although you may attempt to fall back into it to avoid responsibility, I will not respond, and you will be left to a folly of your own making.

EPHESIANS 4:14–16

A SECRET PROCESS

Examine your own relationship to Me and live with Me in the full acceptance of responsibility at that level. If you fall back into childish behavior, your own foolishness will be your punishment, and eventually your folly will be hid from none. Live close to Me, and I will minister to you in secret and do a deep inner work veiled to the eye of man. Others may view the RESULTS, but the process will be secret. When you were in the child stage, it was just the opposite. Others saw the outward discipline, and I saw the inner result. To the casual observer, My choicest saints often appear to escape chastening. But I am dealing with them in a realm of perfecting inner beauty of the soul, as Esther was prepared to meet the king by a full year of cosmetic routine (Esther 2:12). I am doing a similar thing with My Church in this hour, for truly, My Bride is undergoing her beautification in anticipation of the coming of the Bridegroom.

This is why she must be drawn aside. This is not a work accomplished in public. It is a ministry to her inner soul, and I have ordained special ones to carry out this work of preparing the Bride. They are humble, quiet, dedicated servants, yes, they are your angels of mercy, and I commend you into their hands, and may you submit yourself to their ministrations. Only so can you come forth in that day when you would be presented before the King, truly made ready to stand in His presence, purged of flaws and imperfections and all that would mar your beauty in My eyes. For I am more discerning than the eye of man, and that which man looks upon and admires as beauty may utterly fall short in My eyes.

See that you are not deceived by the estimates of others. Pray that you may be fully prepared to meet My discerning gaze.

EPHESIANS 5:27

71

ATTITUDE DETERMINES OUTCOME

In every situation, you have a confrontation of duty. You can, by total dedication of your own being, turn EVERY experience into a spiritual victory. It is the attitude with which you approach any day that will determine its outcome.

You are not a helpless pawn on a board. You are a child of God with prerogatives for accomplishing *His will*, NOT YOUR OWN. Let this help to bring you guidance when you are in doubt.

Be about your Father's business. There will always be plenty of other people occupied with the affairs of the world.

ACTS 26:19

THE SINGING HEART

Patience, My children, will manifest where hope is nurtured. The singing heart is blind to obstacles and recognizes in all things the loving hand of an all-wise Father. In such a state, delays are unnoticed, for the spirit is not bound by the limitations of outer circumstances. The power of evil to destroy joy is nullified when Christ Himself becomes the one point of attention. In Him all things are possessed NOW. . .all things are complete NOW. . .for faith beholds that which is yet to be as though it were already a reality.

Withdraw your attention from the outer circumstance and lose yourself, My child, in the free-flowing stream of the Spirit. Every mountain shall be brought low and the trees shall clap their hands. I will restore, I will bless, and I will heal. Gladness shall be

your daily portion, and joy your meat and drink. I will bless you as
you bless all others and wait only upon Me for your help.

DISAPPOINTMENT

Out of every disappointment there is to be gleaned some
treasure. The enemy would whisper "all is lost." I say to you,
much can be gained.

Refuse the temptation to brood over what is gone. It has
passed into the area of My sovereignty. The PRESENT challenge
requires your undivided attention.

Give no time to dark thoughts. Depression undermines the
vigor of the soul.

LUKE 9:60–62

ON COPING *with* SUCCESS

Be never entangled by thoughts concerning the reactions of
others to your ministry. No decision should EVER be made on this
basis. MINISTER, and follow the leading of the Spirit. The results
will be according to your faith and according to your "dying."
Search your heart, and pray for the strength to receive great results.

I may withhold blessings because in My love and wisdom I
foresee your own unreadiness to receive. Learn how to prepare

your mind and heart to cope with success, otherwise when it comes you may by your very unreadiness and lack of fortitude undo the good which has been done.

MATTHEW 13:11–12

OUTER BLESSING *and* INNER STRENGTH

Ponder for a moment what great crises would face you if tomorrow all your prayers were answered! Could you bear it? . . . the new joy—the added responsibility? Therefore, when you pray, ask not only for the desired results, but also that your heart will be strengthened to receive, and that added wisdom be given to meet the new problems.

You have watched some succeed only to fail. This occurs when outer blessings are sought and inner strength neglected. The two must be combined, and the greater potential is involved in the blessing, the more subsequent fortitude will be required. Otherwise, you will reach the goal and having done so will faint at the self-same spot.

NUMBERS 14:24

KINDNESS

In tenderness, My child, lies the greatest strength that can come to the human heart. Kindness is like a rose, which though easily crushed and fragile, yet speaks a language of silent power. It is the same power that lies in the eyes of one who loves. It is the power that moves the hand of him who gives alms.

Beauty comes to the inner soul of a man as tenderness becomes his outer expression. He who finds it has captured the atmosphere of heaven and has brought to his human relationships the essence of God's holy love. Never shall he search for peace, for he creates within his own heart a pool of restfulness because his every attitude is benevolent. Nothing on earth can shatter his joy, because God's Spirit within his own soul has become his source of happiness, and he is ever richer in sharing. None who look to him are denied, because the love of God embraces all. Gentleness has become his language, and kindness his speech. Christ is the expression of his life, and He has become his deliverer from all that offends His grace.

My Spirit Lights *the* Path

Peace, My child, is in living in My revealed will. What I have spoken to you plainly, for that you are responsible. As you walk in obedience, MORE will be shown, but you will not find peace by demanding to know more but by following the guidance you have already been given.

If in your heart you truly desire to please Me, you have sufficient wisdom for this day, because My Spirit lights the path of him who loves Me, and if you want to please Me it is because you love Me.

Go in joy and in confidence, knowing that I go with you, and as you go I enable you to walk in My grace.

1 JOHN 5:2–3

VIGILANCE

It is vigilance, My child, that keeps the soul from destruction. At no time are you protected from the vicious attacks of evil forces except as you are actively claiming in faith your position in Christ. There is nothing to guard your soul from the devil except the shed blood of Christ. There is the Christian's armor (Ephesians 6:11–18) but each piece, from the helmet of salvation to the sandals of the gospel of peace is dependent upon the finished work of the Lord Jesus Christ upon the cross.

It is in the atonement that you have protection, and only in the blood is power over sin. Never move away from the cross, My child. If you would keep your soul from evil, you must stay beneath its cleansing flow. This is vigilance. You cannot guard nor keep yourself. Only the power of the Holy Ghost can draw you continually into this place. All the enticements of the world and appetites of the carnal nature will draw you out. My Spirit, if you do not resist Me, will draw you in.

Vigilance is your part. Watch which force is drawing you. . . My Holy Spirit, or the spirit of the world. Nothing good ever comes out of *you*. Good comes only out of Me. I am in you as you abide in Me, and I will bring forth My own good through you. It is a moment-by-moment choosing, and death and life are in each choice.

1 PETER 5:8

SINGLENESS *of* MIND

Do you *truly* love Me, My child? Are you genuinely desirous of doing My will? I say unto you, heaven and earth are moved to help when your heart is set on pleasing Me.

Over and over I have pleaded with My people, that they might know the value of singleness of mind, for it is the secret of victory. I may ask great things or small. I judge you not by the scope of influence. . .how important your actions are in the sight of men, but by your purity of motive and the degree of dedication you apply to the task.

Nothing should obscure the revelation of My will. You desire to know: I desire to reveal. Only be mindful that to know My will and not perform it brings severer judgment than to be ignorant.

When you seek Me for guidance, it is actually an expression of love. Failure, then, to fulfill My demands is a denial of that same love which you have voluntarily expressed. Better it is not to profess, than having professed, to deny. I accept your *words;* but you are judged by your *actions.* I accept the profession of your love; but you betray your own heart by disobedience.

JOHN 13:17

The Straight Path

Do not go the way of the world, for it is a pathway strewn with pitfalls. I would lead you in paths of righteousness. It is a STRAIGHT path that leads to life. I will be your protection against the evil force that would draw you into a divergent path or tempt you to desert.

HEBREWS 12:13

Gratitude Frees

Any expression of gratitude refines the soul. To receive a blessing and feel no impulse to express appreciation is the mark of a reprobate. Gratitude is synonymous with My love, for the essence of holy love is the same both when it gives and when it receives. It gives not selfishly and receives not as unto itself. It is a continual flowing out. Therefore, he who receives a blessing in My Spirit will in the very receiving return again a blessing to the giver and will not take unto himself the gift. His gratitude will bless and free both the gift and the giver. He who gives to such a one will find himself enriched, and he who receives in this spirit will multiply all his good.

COLOSSIANS 3:15

An Invisible Shield

My child, My love, My little one; My heart longs to draw you close to Me. Many distractions in the world turn your thoughts away from Me, but I love you with a full attention, like a steady beam of light blazing down upon you.

If you do not feel My love, it is because you are giving your thoughts to other things and other people. They will not only take your attention but will draw on your spiritual energies. They can take from you, but they cannot GIVE to you, and so in each experience you are further impoverished. I alone am the source of life, and unless you seek Me and wait upon Me, you will weaken and sicken, and yes, even die for want of vitality. The more you serve Me, the more this is true.

I am not in the whirlwind of activity, but in the still, small voice of communion. Find it, My child, and hold to it, and you will be energized, and it will protect you like an invisible shield around your soul.

PSALM 28:7

Ask Great Things

Be of good cheer; I have overcome the world.

JOHN 16:33

In every place where I call you to go, there will I be in the midst, ministering of My Spirit, saving, healing, and delivering.

I will not desert you in the place of need or of service. If you are obedient in doing My will, I will never fail to uphold you and strengthen you.

Why do you falter? Heaven's gates are open to your cry. Ask of Me great things. Lo, have I not promised to give BEYOND all you ask or think? Ask in patience, waiting My time of fulfillment.

EPHESIANS 3:20

SPIRITUAL RICHES

Rejoice in Me, for truly I am all you need. I am light and life, hope and peace. I am the joy-giver. My presence is with you, and wherever I am, there is harmony. I am your deliverer and the source of all your strength. You can never ask beyond My power to provide.

Ask then, with complete confidence, but in all you desire, let it be for the enrichment of your soul. Seek not the treasures of the world, for they are transient.

Learn the value of *spiritual* riches, and set your heart to their attainment. You may rightly covet My spiritual gifts. You may lay your natural talents aside and know that as I bestow upon you spiritual enablements, I will use in a new way and in accordance with My highest purposes whatever lies within you of native abilities, or I may give you something entirely new. Nothing is wasted in the Spirit. Much that you do is of less importance in itself than it is as a tool in My hand to shape your eternal soul.

PHILIPPIANS 4:19

FREEBORN *by* GRACE

Christ has redeemed you from the curse of sin. Rejoice, therefore, that you are no longer a slave, but you are freeborn by grace. Walk in this liberty, for as you claim your freedom, it shall become a reality. You have been washed in the blood of the Lamb: Put away, then, all unrighteousness. You have been given a new name: Walk worthy of Him whose name you now bear. You have a new Father: Live in obedience to His will. You have been brought out of bondage: Do not return.

Compromise grieves the Spirit, and rebellion destroys fellowship. Be one of those whose vision is not blurred by selfishness, whose eye is single, and whose heart is without guile.

The humble shall know My Salvation, because they look not to their own strength. All that is noble is placed in man by the hand of the Father. Believe Me to place in you the virtue you most lack in your own nature.

COLOSSIANS 1:10–14

WAIT *and* REJOICE

Be not weary in well doing. It is your Father's good pleasure to give you the kingdom (Luke 12:32). Do not be disheartened if it seems to be delayed in coming. Lo, He is not slack concerning His promises, as some men count slackness. His times are not your times, and His patience endures forever. He can wait and not be anxious. While you see delay, He sees His will being performed in ways not discernable to your eye. What you see as standing still, He sees unfolding. It is like the rose that opens, but the motion is imperceptible to the human eye.

Rest in Him. He is surely bringing to pass His perfect will in and through the entire situation, and it is doing a unique work in many different lives, as they are touched and affected by the action.

Be still and wait. You shall know that the Lord your God, He it is who fights for you, and He will do a miracle before your eyes if you will but trust Him completely and cease to be anxious. What others are doing is as nothing compared to what He is doing and is GOING to do.

REJOICE! Let this be a day of gladness and of jubilation, for our God is mighty, and His hand is working a victory!

PSALM 31:15-24

RELEASE YOUR TENSIONS

The path to holiness is strewn with many heartaches. I bring you through victoriously, but I do not promise that you will escape suffering. It is not by outward joy that the soul is strengthened, nor by physical comfort that the heart is consoled. The reward of righteousness is health and peace; and the self-sacrificing spirit reaps eternal joys.

When you are rebuffed and bear it patiently, yes, even in the moment when it appears as though the actions of others prevent the fulfillment of your own inner vision, be assured, My child, of

My understanding and patience, and know that I am a harmonizing influence.

Even your zeal to please Me should never destroy another, though he appears to block your path of dedication. Bless him, and know that it is possible that he may be fulfilling My purposes for him even though it seems he is hindering your own spiritual expression. I have a unique plan for EACH life, and as you release to Me your tensions, you can rely on Me to continue My work in each soul and bring it ultimately to perfection.

ISAIAH 32:17

PRIDE

Stand firm in your convictions against the contrary wind. EVERY soul struggles against the elements. Thoughts of others can come upon you like a storm at sea until your boat is well-near swamped. Except for My grace, it would be destroyed. But I am near at hand. Listen for MY voice, and heed not the voice of the stranger. Purify your heart so that I can be glorified in all your thoughts and actions.

I am concerned for your victory. You may have it as you fall back into My arms and cease struggling. The struggle enters at the point of the ambitions of the flesh. Many people believe that in serving Me they are free of fleshly exaltation, but this is not necessarily true. Pride will penetrate into the church as surely as into the world.

Guard your heart from false values, and beware when man begins to scheme and promote. I am not in it, says the Lord.

GALATIANS 5:17

A FRESH MOVE *of* FAITH

Praise the Lord; publish His greatness; for He has lifted your burden, He has healed your wound, He has directed your heart toward understanding. He has become your treasure. Your heart shall know peace and gladness because of the presence of your God. Evil shall not plague you, for you walk in love.

Believe Me for the new things. Venture forth in trust. It is time to thrust forward in a new spearhead, a fresh move of faith. Fight procrastination as you would resist evil, for surely it is the enemy of good.

Put forth your hand to the plow and look not back, neither count the cost. I will repay you in the currency of eternity. Keep your eyes on Jesus and walk humbly. Let your words be few and trust the Holy Spirit to speak for Himself. You are not to doctor the souls of others but introduce them to the Great Physician and provide a spiritually healthy atmosphere for those who seek help.

LUKE 9:62

MY HEALING POWER

O My child, take My hand and I will lead you out of the valley. Darkness and shadows are behind you, but light and sunshine are ahead; for I shall bring you into new life and give health, as you have never had it before. I will give vigor and radiant joy. Did I not promise to give "abundant life"? You shall forget the days of illness in the joy of victory; for I not only give you a wonderful victory, but I, your Lord and Saviour, shall Myself become your victory. I have defeated already the foe that wars against you, and My personal experience of triumph I share with you, and we shall rejoice together, for you are My favored child.

Be not afraid with any fear. My love surrounds you, and My power preserves and protects you. My love is perfect, and it is a love that *perfects* and destroys all fear. Lean on Me and trust Me wholly. You will find Me strong and faithful and will be lifted into My arms of unfathomable peace.

I will give you the strength to witness to others of My healing power. You shall be a messenger of hope to those who despair, and you shall bear a word of faith to those who doubt. Your life shall be in My hand, for I have delivered you from destruction and have bound you to My heart in a covenant of holy love. My Spirit shall be upon you, and My blessing go with you wherever you go.

You shall know joy such as the world can never give. There is a rest and a joy which I have reserved for only those who walk with Me. . .for those who listen to My voice and follow in obedience. My way is not difficult: It is blessed. It will not be lonely, for I will be wonderfully near. It is a life of joy, and this joy shall truly be your source of energy, your strength, and your health.

PSALM 103:1–5

INATTENTION

If you will hearken unto Me, I will reveal Myself. I am gracious and patient, but I am grieved by your hardness of heart and inattention. Open rebellion usually brings immediate punishment. *Inattention* can be even more destructive to the soul, because it often goes unnoticed and unrepented and is a secret, unexposed sin.

Cast it out in Jesus' Name, and refuse the robber who would take your dearest treasure. . .your singleness of heart in your love for Me.

LUKE 11:34–36

POSSESS *the* LAND

There is a day coming when you will desire to search My Word and the privilege will be denied. Tarry not for a more convenient season, for the hour is late and many are hungering, and you can be used as a channel if you will present yourself to Me as a living sacrifice. To be sure, it *is* a sacrifice. Any ministry in the Spirit takes its toll in physical energy and requires the giving up of personal comfort; but the rewards are of eternal value, and the joy and satisfaction shall be great.

Contact those who are skilled in breaking the bread of life. You need do little more than give Me the opportunity to work. The results shall be astonishing, and you will say, "Surely this is by the hand of the Lord!"

Move in and possess your inheritance, for verily the shadows are falling across a land that has known light and has rejected it and chosen to walk in darkness.

Strengthen the saints and support one another in the Lord that you may be able to endure the times of testing.

1 THESSALONIANS 5:11–24

DO NOT GATHER FIRE

Can a man take fire in his bosom, and his clothes not be burned?
PROVERBS 6:27

Have I not said that you should pray much that you might not enter into temptation? You are in My care at all times, but there are some stresses put upon the soul that could be avoided by not presuming upon My grace.

He who would not fall off the precipice must not venture too near the edge. Many a soul is placed in jeopardy by folly. Pray for wisdom and avail yourself of every natural protection. This also is My grace at work within you, causing you to desire not to expose the soul to situations which would tend to set the stage for sin.

I desire always to help, but many pray too late; for by their own careless actions they have placed their own feet in a slippery path, and the results are almost inevitable. Prayer at this point is like seeking guidance when the route has been predetermined by self-will and the destination is already in sight.

I will keep you in peace, but ONLY when your mind is stayed upon Me (Isaiah 26:3).

I will order the steps of the man who has made GOODNESS his rule of life (Psalm 37:23).

I will give rest to those who COME to Me (Matthew 11:28).

It is written: *"Resist the devil, and he will flee from you"* (James 4:7). I will not drive the devil away from you; YOU must RESIST him. I will keep your soul from bitterness as you LOVE your ENEMIES. I will make you like a flourishing tree planted by the river of righteousness IF you do not walk in the counsel of the ungodly (Psalm 1:1–3).

I AID you toward holiness, but I will never FORCE anyone to keep My commandments. I have told you that they are GOOD, and those who keep them are happy (Proverbs 29:18). The choice is yours.

Do not gather fire into your garments and pray not to be burned nor take up a serpent and ask for protection. Give the devil wide berth, and in so doing spare the soul much unnecessary anguish.

LEARN *to* LISTEN

When you pray, My child, do not make it a one-way conversation. Know that I am listening, but know also that *I will respond and will speak to you if you give Me opportunity*. Prayer is

not only of the lips, but of the ear also, for prayer is of the
HEART, and the heart that has learned to love has learned to listen—yes, *to listen more than to speak!* Man has been given two
ears and only one tongue that he might perceive that he ought
to LISTEN twice as much as he speaks.

A loving heart will teach you this. Speaking is often motivated
by self-seeking, self-preservation, self-defense, self-aggrandizement,
and every other expression of the ego. Listening is an expression of
interest and concern for others. You reveal weakness of character
and spiritual immaturity when you come to Me filling all the
silences with a verbose recital of your personal desires and with
pious phrases designed to impress Me and gain My approval.

When you come to Me in prayer, you ought to come to
ENJOY Me, not to entertain Me. It is a lack of humility that
causes you to be verbally expansive.

PROVERBS 10:19

A HOLY TEMPLE

Your heart, My child, is the citadel of the Holy Spirit. No
evil shall dwell there as long as you allow Me to rule and reign. I
hold the keys to every chamber and will keep out every evil
thing if you do not invite the enemy. I desire for you a holy temple. I will drive out of your soul all that offends Me, even as I
drove the money changers and the sellers of doves from My
Father's house, and for the same reasons. I desire that *your*

house, like the holy temple, should be a house of prayer. You cannot entertain traffic with unrighteousness and injustice and at the same time maintain an atmosphere of prayer.

Those who sold doves I expelled as well as the money changers. Ah, My child, there are many today who are "selling doves" in places that had been dedicated to worship. Compromise has invaded the sanctuary, and those who serve Me only with lip service presume to attend My altars.

Let not your worship be tinged with carnality. Give Me your adoration from a pure heart and let no ulterior motives invade your personal sanctuary, for I desire truth in the depths of the soul and the divided heart cannot worship.

PSALM 24:3–5

THE COWARD SEEKS RELEASE

Hold fast, My child, for in the hour of anguish, THEN shall you walk in victory. Do not pray to be brought out of the fire until AFTER you have found Me real in the midst of it.

The coward seeks release from pressure. The courageous pray for strength to overcome the evil force.

DANIEL 3:27

I WILL NOT COUNT *the* COST

God's ways are best
His hand doth guide
I follow unafraid
He knows the future
As the past. . .
I will not be dismayed.

It matters not
The steep ascent
I will not count the cost
I'll mark the path
My Saviour went
To seek and save the lost.

'Tis not for me
To know the end,
One step is all He shows.
My constant prayer
That in His love
My soul may find repose.

Thus shall I rest
And know full well
Whatever else betide,
He has a gift
To share with those
Who in His love abide.

F J R

Vision Versus Dreams

No sacrifice should be looked upon as such if it is made for My glory. You shall not count the suffering endured for My sake. You shall suffer and forget and sacrifice with no thought of the price. My blessing should be of more value to you than ALL your possessions, and yes, even more than your aspirations and ideals, for these are still expressions of the desire of the ego for fulfillment.

In My Spirit there can be no cherishing of personal dreams. They must be put to death whenever they are detected. Only the doing of the Father's will is to be sought, and there is a vast difference between a God-inspired vision and personal dreams and aspirations.

PHILIPPIANS 3:8

Sacrifice

Then shall ye know, if ye follow on to know the LORD.

HOSEA 6:3

If you follow on with Me, My child, you will come to know a peace of heart impossible to find anywhere except in the place of full dedication to My will. You will find here a joy the like of which the world cannot know. Yes, you will find strength; for out of purity of heart comes courage. Because you love Me, *the difficult shall be easy and the natural impossible.*

Circumstances that bind the coward are to the strong but an opportunity to rise as a bird rises on the wings of the wind. It is selfishness that keeps the coward a prisoner to his fears, and it is love that makes the brave man rise above his challenges, spurning even the awareness of his sacrifices.

Yes, *"the difficult shall be easy,"* for when I ask you to sacrifice for Me, you shall do it gladly. And *"the natural shall be impossible,"* for what you would be prone to do if you yielded to natural inclination, you will flee from without a backward glance rather than grieve Me. For love seeks not her own, and to please Me you will sacrifice your personal wishes whenever they run counter to My highest purposes for your life. But if you *fully* follow Me, I will take you into places in the walk of obedience that will enrich your soul and bless your life far beyond any pleasure the world can offer.

Come with Me, My beloved, come with Me to the mountain of spices. . .to the place where sacrifice for My sake becomes sweet and loss is gain. Yes, to gain is to lose if in gaining it is Me that you have lost. And to lose is to gain if it is a closer fellowship with Me that is gained.

You will not count the cost in terms of sacrifice if you truly love Me. Until you love Me "more than these," you will continue to fail. But I will bring you out of failure and into victory as you seek Me above all else and love Me beyond all others.

MARK 8:34–38

TRIBULATION

Through much tribulation I am bringing My chosen to perfection. Be not amazed when challenges present themselves. I am building your fortitude, and the day will come when you will be grateful for every lesson learned in the school of affliction.

1 PETER 4:12

ANXIETY

My child, when you are tired, do not be disheartened. Most of your discouragement comes when you carry your own burden, forgetting to call upon Me for help. Give Me everything, and quickly; for as soon as any heaviness of spirit sets in, trust is crowded out. An atmosphere of anxiety or unhappiness is withering to faith.

Continual prayer will fortify your soul.

ROMANS 12:12

TRIM YOUR WICK

O My child, do not that which I have not bidden. I prepare the way when I thrust you out, but if man has called, you venture forth unprotected.

It is in My Name alone that you ought to minister, and only when your own soul is free can the Spirit move unhindered. No peace can come to your heart or to others when you are moving outside My will. Make no mistake about it: These things are not concealed in the Spirit, and even the babe in Christ is able to discern between the moving of the Spirit and the empty action of the flesh, even when the flesh is attempting to serve God.

Not only is time wasted when you disobey Me, but many souls are damaged, and your own no less.

Never try to evaluate a situation. Obey Me. It is difficult only to be obedient. How can you presume to handle any more? When you have difficulty finding My will, how can you feel capable of making judgments concerning others?

Trim your wick and polish your lamp. Your light is growing dim. Come back to listening only to My voice, and refuse ever to follow another though he be the greatest of saints.

I love you, and I have chosen and trained you to do the tasks I have ordained. Be content with nothing less.

PSALM 139:23–24

THE ROMANCE *of the* SPIRIT

There is a path of service in which I would lead you where the grass is green, the pastures verdant. No foot has preceded you there. It is virgin territory. You shall walk with ME because there is none other gone before to mark the way. It is My own special

95

way for you. It is a way of romance—the Romance of the Spirit.

My love for you is deeper than you have comprehended. As you walk on into fuller commitment, and as you are less hampered by the things of the world, I will give you deeper insight and more complete revelations of Myself.

Your nature needs refining. Your will needs to be bent yet more. Your conformity to My purposes is not complete. When you have given up EVERYTHING, we will be able to go forth TOGETHER, and you will experience an inner power that you were not able to find before.

PSALM 119:1–6

HOLD YOUR GROUND

I have not brought you out of the wilderness to allow you to be devoured by the giants in the land. I brought you out by a miracle of My divine grace, and I bring you in that you may experience My delivering power as you are confronted by the enemy in all his varied strategy and devices.

Stretch forth the hand of faith. Set foot upon the territory you wish to claim. I will move ahead of you and clear a path, but you must be determined to follow closely and to hold your ground without wavering.

NUMBERS 13:30, 14:8

Fear, *a* Sin

Be not faint of heart. Fear will rob you of your possession as quickly as any other sin; for truly fear is a sin and it opens the door for many other sins to follow.

Guard your heart from doubt and every negative attitude. You cannot afford to take the risk of entertaining any such thoughts at so critical a time. Only the strong in faith shall prevail. Only those with a "Caleb" spirit shall take the walled cities and crush out the enemies.

NUMBERS 14:24

Concentration

Give your full strength to the conflict. Think of nothing else. Only concentration brings results. Lo, the enemy is concentrating against you to destroy you. You will have to bring a stronger force to bear against him if you hope to escape, much less defeat him.

Gird on your armor, for the battle is not against flesh and blood, but against principalities and powers and against spiritual forces of darkness intruding into sacred places. I am at your side to help you.

EPHESIANS 6:12

RECOGNIZE *the* ENEMY

O My child, hear My voice, and let not the crafty words of a stranger influence your thinking. My Word is all you need. Study it more and be filled with its wisdom that you may be fortified against insidious attacks of fallacious human reasonings. The high-sounding phrases of the humanist seem convincing at times, especially those times when you are in a condition of weariness and in a place of testing and searching. But I say to you that any search that leads you to your own self rather than to Me is of the devil. Either take the offensive and win a victory for Me, or else sever the connection with that one who is walking in the darkness of his own reasoning mind. It would be better to retreat than to fall into a snare. You may be better prepared at a later time. You have a full-scale assignment already at hand and need all your resources for this.

Recognize the attempt of the enemy to distract you from concentration, and refuse it. Shake off the viper, as Paul on the Island of Malta (Acts 28:1–6). This will strengthen your witness, even as it did for the apostle, and open the door for the proclamation of the truth to those to whom you have been sent.

2 CORINTHIANS 6:14–18

THE COMFORT *of* MY PRESENCE

Over and over have I reassured you of My love for you. More than all the comforts of the world, I want you to know the comfort of My presence in such a way that you will never again question My reality nor doubt My concern for you.

Many dangers beset your path, but I shall keep you if you trust in Me. Many sorrows compass you about, but I give you joy that is greater. Darkness presses you, and doubts arise, but My light, the light of My Holy Spirit, ever burns within your heart to cheer you and encourage you to go on, yes, to go on knowing surely I will bring you out.

PSALM 18:27-35

HESITATION

Never delay My blessing by indecision. I can only fill that which you give Me. If you do not ACT in response to My directives, you will never receive My enablement.

I give you strength according to the task, but I give it *as you do the work*. To hesitate is to become still more weak and timid, for it is a sense of inadequacy that causes you to draw back and fear to move, and this draws your attention to yourself; and because there is never sufficient power within yourself to do the Father's work, any focus on your own strength or ability will soon persuade you that the task is impossible.

PHILIPPIANS 4:13

LOOSE *the* CHILD

The little ones are in My care; you shall not be anxious. It is written that He carries the lambs in His bosom. Surely, it is true. Rely on Me for I am ever watchful, and the tenderness of My love exceeds that of a mother.

Picture the Lord Jesus as He took the young children upon His knee and blessed them, placing His hands upon their heads. I say to you, He is the same today, and His compassion fathomless. Trustingly place your child in His hands. They are *healing* hands, and you may count on Him to bring wholeness and perfection, whether here or in the Father's house.

Your heart is bound to the heart of the child. Loose the cord of affection lest it break. You need to commit all to Him, otherwise your heart will not only be grieved but torn. You shall not only weep but bleed. But I would not have it so. I am not only a healer of bodies but a healer of hearts also, and I shall administer to you a full measure of comfort if you will allow Me to draw near.

PSALM 55:22

HEED MY WORDS

The faithful are listening for My voice, and only Mine. I say to you, give heed to My words. They shall be health to your soul and your daily sustenance. They are sent not to bind, but to free; not to discourage, but to give you strength. Truly, they are life.

They shall be so to you, and they shall become a quickening power as you speak them to others.

Know My message for TODAY. Wait upon Me until you find it. Let not the voices of men deflect you from walking in My will. Obedience is precious to Me, and when you have a pliable spirit, you give Me pleasure.

So many of My children do not listen, and because they do not make an effort to hear Me, they are caught in the snare of being controlled by the voices which are shouting in the world about them.

I alone can give you the wisdom you need, and man can help you only if he is a channel for My message. If you are ministered to by one who is speaking in the Spirit, give heed to that message, and test it by the Holy Scriptures, and let it do its work in your soul; but do not lay yourself open to idle conversation, thereby weakening your spiritual life.

Walk in the Spirit; pray in the Spirit; think the thoughts that flow from the mind of Christ; fellowship and speak to HIM. Do not continue to seek companionship with those who are walking in the way of the world. For the world shall pass away and the lusts thereof, but the Word of the living God abideth forever.

1 JOHN 2:17

THE RIGHTEOUS REMNANT

Hear Me, O My people, and listen to My words. You give attention continually to the words of men. You listen, read, you study and ponder and consider multitudes of words that express only the thoughts of others who, like yourself, are searching for Truth. To search is not evil, but if you desire understanding, come directly to Me. Ask of Me. As the Scriptures teach, if any seeks wisdom, let him ask of God, for He gives liberally (James 1:5).

Wait upon Me, and I will clarify things that are dark and puzzling to you. Israel is My chosen people now as truly as in days of old, but like My Church has failed Me, even so has My people, Israel. There is, as there has always been, a wide discrepancy between what I have taught them, yes, even between what they BELIEVE, and what they experience. . .what they accept as My commandments, and what they DO. You have BOTH fallen short, Church and Israel alike.

But I shall have a people. Yes, I shall have MANY, even in this day. I shall have those in whom I can rejoice as I found pleasure in the devotion of David and in the integrity of Job; yes, in the faith of the Shunamite, and the courage of Elijah. These lived in times when those who were truly dedicated to Me were in the minority, even as today. Goodness has never been a common commodity. Devotion and self-sacrifice have always been at a premium.

I shall have a people. . .but it will be the righteous remnant. It will be no larger, percentage wise, than the family of Noah in the days of the flood.

ROMANS 9:26–29

Love Endures

Through many bewildering experiences I deal with the soul of a man. When there is submission of spirit, all things work together for good. This is why I said all things work together for good to them that love Me (Romans 8:28). The soul that submits to My disciplines is the soul that loves Me. Love will hold a man steady beneath the chastening rod because love believes and hopes in all things (1 Corinthians 13:7). Love will never fail. It will endure whatever comes because it rests in Me rather than in the circumstance.

It is by My spirit that you overcome, because My Spirit is the spirit of love, for God is love; and love will give tolerance for hardship. He who knows he is loved can be content with a piece of bread, while all the luxuries of the world cannot satisfy the craving of the lonely.

You need never be that one deprived of comfort as long as your desires are fulfilled in Me; for as it is written, I satisfy the hungry with good things, while the rich go empty away (Luke 1:53). He who goes away will always be empty in spite of his riches. He who seeks Me will never be unhappy or poor.

The Quiet Spirit

Be silent when you come to Me. Only the quiet spirit enters the place of communion. Strivings are left outside. Vexations bar the door, for they are caused by reactions to things, places, and people, and none of these are related to worship. They are related to the flesh man. Put them out of the temple. They that have clean hands and a pure heart shall ascend unto the mountain of the Lord. When you are loosed from the earthly, then shall the heavenly be revealed.

PSALM 24:3–5

THE DOOR IS OPEN

My child, the door is open. You shall go through by My grace and in My strength. Never gauge the possibilities of victory by examining your own strength. I am your Life, your Purity, your Wisdom, and your Strength. You have built faith for many years through a knowledge of and confidence in My Word. *Now,* I say unto you, Put it into operation by WALKING in the path of action. Only in this way can you come into the full possession of your inheritance. It is not for the fearful, this walk of faith—it is for the courageous. . . even the reckless soul.

Move out, and trust Me as you go. Trust not yourself. Lean not on past experiences. Look not to friends for advice and support. Look to ME. It is My work that I am asking you to do, so it is I who will direct you and provide your needs.

Give Me your yieldedness, your love, and a pure desire. I will do the rest.

1 CORINTHIANS 16:9

SEERS

There is a spirit of bewilderment abroad in the land today that causes people to go about as though they were moving through a dense fog. Vision is obscured. Never have I needed watchmen, heralds, prophets, and seers as I need them in this hour.

Stay close to Me no matter what attractions exert themselves to draw you away. I need more time with you, and you need to give fuller attention to the things of the Spirit.

You can never fail to hear My voice if your ears have been unstopped by obedience and the desire to please and serve Me.

LUKE 8:18

ON PRIVACY

Do not allow your thoughts to pursue in curiosity what you do not understand in the lives of others. Much mischief can come thus upon your own soul, and nothing good will be accomplished. Count it a sacred trust to guard and maintain the sanctity of life.

To violate the spiritual privacy of another is a greater breach of ethics than to invade his house uninvited. Rest assured that if your friendship warrants, he will share with you as he deems wise, and what he appears to withhold, you will (if your affection for him is genuine) have the confidence that he is withholding as much for your own good as for his.

Love believes only the best.* There is no more eloquent way to express love and respect for another than by allowing him full liberty of independent action.

*1 CORINTHIANS 13:4–7

STRENGTH *and* WEAKNESS

Christ Jesus. . .is made unto us wisdom, and righteousness,
and sanctification, and redemption:
That, according as it is written,
He that glorieth, let him glory in the Lord.

1 CORINTHIANS 1:30–31

My Spirit within you, My child, is the source of your spiritual life and strength. Look not to your own natural abilities, for My Spirit empowers the one who would walk in faith, so that he who is weak need not despair, and he who feels himself to be strong shall learn not to boast; for I bring down the mighty and make strong the weak.

PROTECTION

My protection is all you need, My child. The help of man is vain, for he who would protect another is himself never beyond the reach of danger. He who looks to the Almighty for aid will not be tempted to seek elsewhere for strength or shelter.

Information man may supply, but bring this to Me, and let Me give you wisdom as to the right use of knowledge. All will fall into place beautifully as you rest it in My hands. Fear not that any can harm you. Fear only the potential treachery of your own heart, for often in the midst of what seems a holy action, there suddenly appears a traitorous motive.

Seek guidance for outer action, but be even more concerned with the desires of the heart, that they be consistent with the character of the Lord Jesus Christ. Never did He call upon men for protection, nor even upon angels, although they were sent to minister to Him. It was His own inner unification with the Father's heart that effected His preservation against all evil that was directed against Him. Even so, your own heart purity determines the extent of your personal preservation.

In the biblical account (2 Kings 6:17) Gehazi owed his own safety to Elisha, for God was with Elisha, the man of God, in the form of an angelic host that filled the mountains, and Gehazi, the servant, benefited by being in his company. So shall it be for those who journey with you, as God, seeing your confidence in Him and desire to please Him and do His will, moves in your behalf.

Cast fear forever from your heart. God's love protects the sparrow: Surely He is near His children who rely on His faithfulness!

Let My peace fill your heart, and if ever it is not present, wait in My presence, and go not out until it has been regained. I WILL direct your steps. I WILL provide for your needs. I WILL deliver you from evil. Rely on Me.

1 THESSALONIANS 5:23–24

MAINTAIN CONSTANCY

Do not grieve, My child, though all you hold dear be taken from you. You have need of nothing. You feel that you need something or someone when communion has been neglected. Hold Me close to your heart, and I will satisfy every longing. Allow Me to comfort you, and you will find yourself reaching out less and less to others for support and solace.

My presence will sustain you, but only if you maintain a closeness of relationship. Pure neglect alone can cause you to lose this as much as open sin. Sin is your enemy, to be sure, but so also is indolence and inattention.

Hold fast your faith. Let no man rob you of your reward. Where you go and what you do is not your primary concern. The essential thing is the matter of your heart attitude toward Me.

Maintain a constancy in devotion, and I will be pleased and will do all manner of wonderful things in your behalf. I will cause men to heap blessings upon you. You will be increased abundantly in the riches of the Kingdom.

PSALM 107:9

FAITH REACHES BEYOND

"Whatever you ask in prayer, believe that you receive it, and you will."

MARK 11:24 RSV

Faith, My child, reaches out beyond the need and into the

supply, and always remember that the supply is greater than the need.

Do you need forgiveness? Lo, I have provided enough that if all human souls ever created turned to Me in repentance, they would be fully pardoned. Will I then deem your sins too great for remission?

Do you need power to overcome temptation? Lo, I have overcome, and in Me there is victory for every soul that casts itself upon My mercy.

It is patience for which you pray? Know that in the Spirit there is no time, and that for which you wait is already given and only waits your receiving.

SHARE COURAGE

Your compassion for other souls will be in direct proportion to your own sense of need. Self-dependence makes it difficult to comprehend the timidity of the weak. Though you may have gained a measure of strength, remember that it was not native; it has been cultivated through a multitude of experiences, and you can remember many times when you were fearful and trembling. Other souls are still in the place of fear and desperation. Be always ready and willing to stand with them in that place and share your faith and courage, yes, even as many others shared with *you* in *your* times of need!

1 CORINTHIANS 9:22

GOD'S PURPOSE

God's purpose in making a man holy involves His own glory. He is not waiting to hear a man called holy; He is listening to hear man call *HIM HOLY*. He is not interested in making man a reputation but in making him a disciple. This applies even in the matter of a man achieving a reputation as holy.

The rich young ruler flattered Jesus by addressing Him as "good master," and Jesus rebuked him with the words, "Why callest thou Me good? Only God is good," thus pressing upon him the necessity to decide either to not call him good or to acknowledge His deity. How then can He be pleased that any man would call another man good, or that one should desire such a reputation? To be sure, a man is to desire holiness, but he is not to desire such as a reputation, but for God's glory, and for His alone.

Gone must be the pride in our own goodness.

MATTHEW 19:16–17

TRUE HOLINESS

True holiness, when wrought in a man by the grace of God, is not an end in itself. It is a transforming work effected by the Holy Spirit to the end that God's will may be accomplished through that vessel. His eternal purposes and His ultimate total victory over all evil are ever His vision. The individual vessel either hastens or detains the end result, to his own blessing or detriment as the case may be. If he is a flowing, vital part of God's eternal purpose, he is blessed. If he, by his willful disobedience, becomes a hindering factor, he suffers in accordance to the degree of his rebellion.

ROMANS 12:1–2

THE CALL *of the* SPIRIT

Today is the day of salvation. Tomorrow is not given you to possess. Tomorrow is not a mysterious unknown: It will be the fruitage of what you sow today. Your response to Me at this moment becomes your present experience of salvation. The past cannot be recaptured. Future choices are yet to be made. Your answer to My call at the point where you now find yourself is the one deciding factor.

Regret weakens, and procrastination destroys the vision. Without vision the people perish. He who walks in faith fulfills his own vision. He works out his own salvation as he responds to the call of the Spirit. Flesh will not respond to the Spirit. Flesh responds to flesh. Spirit responds to Spirit. He who follows Me must follow Me in Spirit and in truth.

A false follower is one who follows in the flesh and has not heard the call of the Spirit. Such a one, in his self-energized zeal becomes a hazard on the road of service. He is in defeat by default but judges himself to be successful. He is out of harmony with My will while presuming to know it and teach others.

Repent, all of you. With a whole heart seek My face and My forgiveness. Grace will be given according to the depth of your confession of need.

PHILIPPIANS 2:12-13

KEY *to* JOY

Surrender is the key to joy. By release the soul is freed. Bondage is the twin of selfishness. To hold is to lose, and to free is to gain.

Meditation opens the door to revelation, and revelation brings liberation. Test it in any given situation. You will find that you hold in your own hand the instrument of life. It will work like a magic eye to open the heaviest door.

MARK 8:35-36

IMMEDIATE OBEDIENCE

You never enhance either your own life nor the lives of others if you are out of My perfect will. When I give you guidance and you are persuaded in your own mind of My leading, never ponder your decision. There is but one possible reply, and that is "Yes, Lord." Then simply do My bidding, and do it immediately.

Much confusion and remorse would be averted if all My children acted in this manner. This is why delayed obedience is nearly always DISOBEDIENCE, because along with the procrastination there is deliberation followed by rationalization, and by the time decision finally evolves into action, your own will is in control.

I SAIAH   1 : 19

CONTENTMENT

Many are the afflictions of the righteous:
but the LORD delivereth him out of them all.

P SALM   34:19

My children do not enjoy immunity to trouble, but in the midst of each painful experience My Spirit is at work fashioning beauty in the soul. It matters not how long the day, how steep and hard the road, if only you may see My face and know I bear the load.

Be patient in tribulation and I will minister My grace to you and your heart will rejoice, yes, more than in the day of pleasantness. For when outer blessings are withheld, inner peace is deepened, for the soul turns to worship with less distraction.

Disappointment is foreign to the Spirit, for it has no part in faith. The trusting soul possesses all things in Christ and looks not to man for his blessing: Therefore he can never be disappointed. Joy and contentment crown his head, and peace reigns in his heart.

FREE YOURSELF *of the* GRAVE CLOTHES

O My child, how many times have I spoken to you of the nearness of My coming? Be not disobedient. You have need of the grave clothes being removed; for I would bring you out, even as I brought Lazarus out. I have already delivered you from death, and I have delivered you from the tomb; and now I would have you set free from the binding things with which you were bound when you were once dead. These things have no place in your life anymore. Like the grave clothes, they may have served a purpose in the past, but now that you are alive and have come out into liberty of spirit, you must be liberated in body; for how can your free spirit tolerate a bound body?

Lazarus is a type of My people who have experienced a spiritual resurrection. They are also pictured in Ezekiel's vision of the dry bones. Ezekiel's picture is of the entire body of Christ coming together and being joined in a unit, whereas Lazarus is a picture of the spiritual resurrection of the individual believer.

This is the fourth day, and you are seeing many Lazaruses come forth, yes, is not Christ calling them forth? They are not coming forth in response to the cries of men. They have been awakened from a sleep of death by the voice of God. Deliver them now, and seek deliverance yourself from everything that pertains to death and the grave. Be not entangled again, wrote the Apostle Paul, with any sort of bondage. Get free of all that man has put upon you with the intent of preserving the flesh. This new life I have given you Myself, and I will clothe you in new and beautiful garments. These shall not bind you neither restrict your movement. They shall clothe you as feathers clothe the bird. They shall be so suitable and appropriate for this new life in the Spirit that they shall actually aid your travel. For you must travel swiftly, and you must travel much. Yes, I will send you to places you have never seen before; but you can never go thus until after this great and complete liberation. Great because of the victory over the enemy which is involved, and complete because you shall never go into such captivity again. You will experience a wholly new life and will see many come to Me because of curiosity concerning your resurrection.

Be obedient. Loose yourself and loose others. Fear not where you shall be gathered, for I say unto you, you shall be gathered *unto Myself!* And I will keep you and will add more to your number. Free yourself of the grave clothes of religion so that I may give you the wedding garment.

The dead church needs to be wrapped in something; but I will clothe My people with liberty. If I am to send you as I desire, you must be free physically as well as spiritually. You have no part nor place in the dead church. Come out, and be separated, and touch not the unclean. That is, pertaining to the dead body. Touch not the dead body. You are unclean if you do and need days of cleansing. You will not be ready for My coming unless you come out and purify yourself and make clean your hands.

O death, where is thy sting? O grave, where is thy victory? The sting of death is sin; and the strength of sin is the law. I want you delivered of death *and the grave.* The devil has brought sin, and the apostate church has provided the tomb.

Come forth! Walk with Me in newness of life, in purity of heart, and in freedom of worship!

I am your High Priest, and I am the Bishop of your soul.

TURBULENCE, *a* WARNING SIGNAL

One step at a time, My child. When I lead, there is no confusion. Never let OTHERS lead. Your need for confirmation will be answered by the Spirit. My Holy Spirit meets your every need. If it is wisdom that you seek, you will receive it if you draw upon Him. He resides within you to be your ALL. Never bypass this infinite supply of all good. Never move into a new situation until you are at peace about it within your own soul. If there is disturbance, you will communicate the same to those who work with you, and they will be disheartened. My Spirit harmonizes all action. If you sense discord or turbulence, know that there is a spiritual battle already on the scene. Let it be a warning signal. Look for the root of it, and do not blindly forge ahead until AFTER it is either removed or resolved. It may require more courage than you feel you have, but if you rely on Me, I will give you added grace. To ignore it and push on will spell disaster and demand even more strength to recover your position, much less to make an advance.

I who know all things say to you, My child, that in My will there are many challenges, but there is PEACE. *Do not move when it is not present.*

ROMANS 8:14

116

AFFLICTION, NO STRANGER

Many are the afflictions of the righteous:
but the LORD delivereth him out of them all.

PSALM 34:19

Affliction is no stranger to the child of God. I cannot spare you suffering. Grief and death are the experience of every man, and darkness falls upon both saint and sinner. He who knows Me intimately will find a deep joy in the midst of life's bitterness; and My Spirit dwelling within gives stamina in the face of hardship.

I do not smooth out the way for My loved ones, for how then could they testify of My provision? Better your lips were sealed forever than that they should deny Me in the hour of calamity.

I prepare you in order to USE you in the hour of crisis. The crisis is not the time to cry for *deliverance,* saying, "Lord, *save* me," but to cry, "Lord, *use* me."

JOB 13:15; 23:8-10

TRUST

You struggle, My child, when you could as easily rest in My arms. You concern yourself with the actions of others and neglect the only important thing: to abide in Me. He who abides in Me has no need to be anxious, for he draws from Me strength and peace. In this place of quietness I reveal Myself, and in so doing, the whole atmosphere is charged with faith. Light floods the soul; mercy governs the actions; and all is brought into harmony.

It is when you are moving out of My divine will that you have unrest. Abiding brings confiding, for to know Me is to trust Me, and trust brings peace. Your trust in Me is colored by human experience. This should never be allowed to happen. Though all men fail, I am no less faithful: Indeed, in the face of human disappointments your trust in Me becomes even more vital.

Failure of men is often the instrument of grace in My hand to cause a soul to look to Me in total dependence. Total failure of man often brings total dependence on God. Experience has again brought insight. To understand is to believe, and to believe is to trust.

PSALM 56:11–13

A HEART FIXED *on* ME

As I have told you so often, KEEP YOUR HEART FIXED ON ME. Only thus will you have the needed stamina to keep your own soul from falling into discouragement. Only by My power will you be able to stand. Focus on My footsteps. The ways that other men walk are not your concern. Jesus every day sought the path of the Father's will. Never once was He ever deflected for a moment by the way of life that others were pursuing. So must you do. Walk alone with Me, and although I use you to minister to many, follow none. *Follow Me.*

This is the inmost secret of a holy life: the doing of MY will. The more perfectly you fulfill My will (My SPECIFIC plan for you), the more pleasing you are to Me; and I am more pleased with your obedience than with your understanding, although you have a tendency to be more concerned with the latter! You often seek to understand things that are too complex and things that are not meant for you to know at this time. Be content to know that I have full knowledge, and be willing to wait for the day in which I have promised that the many impenetrable mysteries of life shall be unfolded.

JOB 22:21

HEAVEN'S GIFT

Quietness of soul, My child, is heaven's rarest gift enjoyed aforetime. It is unknown to the sinner, for there is no peace to the wicked, but only stress and restlessness. To abide in Me is to know release from tensions; and the ear that is attuned to My voice does not respond to chaos.

Man assaults his ears with noise to drown the cry of his soul for help. All too often he chooses to perpetuate his own misery rather than repent of his evil ways and accept the rulership of another who is greater than himself.

ISAIAH 32:17–18

THE CROSS *in the* STAR

The CROSS, My child, is *My* symbol of Christmas. Wise men *followed the star,* but it was the SAVIOUR whom they *sought.* Wrapped that holy night in swaddling clothes was My perfect gift to mankind. Cradled in the arms of Mary lay the only hope of man's salvation. Shepherds were drawn to worship Him by the love that flowed through Him as He became the channel for redeeming grace. For *"the Word was made flesh, and dwelt among us, (and we beheld his glory, the glory as of the only begotten of the Father,) full of grace and truth"* (John 1:14).

Small wonder there was an angelic visitation! Marvel, rather, that the entire firmament was not ablaze with holy light, and that all the hosts of angelic beings did not crowd the stable and encompass the whole world that night! For it is written that even the angels longingly desire to enter into the mystery of the redemption of man through the incarnation of Christ (1 Peter 1:12).

Hallowed by His presence were the dusty streets of Bethlehem. Blessed was every man, woman, and child, though they were ignorant of His advent. Singularly favored were those to whom were granted a divine revelation!

And in that hour of the visitation of God to earth, Bethlehem and Calvary were already fused in the heart of God; and all who beheld the star through His eyes saw in its heart the cross.

Yes, 'twas a baby lying in the manger, but within the precious bundle of humanity beat the heart of the creator of the universe and the Saviour of mankind. No power of earth or hell could stop the eternal plan from fulfillment. Grace and mercy became His garments, and darkness was scattered by His feet.

Breathe upon us, O God, the soul-enlightening presence of Thy Holy Spirit until we become those who seek only Christ and follow after Him, bathed in the light of His cross; for only in Calvary do we find the fulfillment of the angelic proclamation of peace on earth, good will toward men; and only in the cross do we discover the triumph of love over hate, peace in place of strife, and light dispelling darkness. Amen.

PHILIPPIANS 2:5–8

UNSEEN COMPANIONSHIP

Courage, My child! No hand shall sustain you but Mine own. Hoped you for another? Disappointment awaits every soul not sustained by My love. Never draw from other sources, for when you do, you rob the life force from another, leaving him weaker and yourself deceived; for you confuse comfort with strength.

Fellowship is not life. It is to be *given* rather than *sought*. It is shared in the overflow. The soul that has been enriched by communion with God will not be dismayed by isolation but will welcome solitude. He will seek not the crowd but the closet and emerging will never walk alone, for he has always unseen companionship, and whoever joins him on the way will be doubly blessed.

PSALM 16

PRETENSE WILL NOT WORSHIP

Out of much solitude comes a depth of understanding I cannot give to the one who pulls the world about himself as a blanket to cover his nakedness or closes himself in with noises to prevent hearing the emptiness of his own soul. Maturity comes in silence, for I am the source of life and wisdom. You shall not learn from men, but from My Spirit. The riches of heaven cannot be purchased from the world. The spiritual man will never be refreshed at the well of carnal reasoning.

Only prayer furnishes the soul with nourishment; but prayer itself must be born of singleness of heart. Pretense will not enter the gate of worship. Pretense will stand outside and flaunt its own self-proclaimed piety. It will not stoop to enter, for it will not part company with false values. Pretense waits for advantage and disdains self-abasement. It thrives on flattery and relishes recognition. Pretense will perform for applause but will reject the obscure task. Pretense has no place in My Kingdom. I would have you true and honest. Better for a man to be a sinner and confess it than to profess a purity he does not possess.

Search your heart in the light of My Word. Let the Holy Spirit give insight.

JOHN 16:13–15

THE MYSTERY *of* RIGHTEOUSNESS

Grace is My abundant mercies showered upon the spiritually destitute. It is the fulness of My love poured out upon the loveless. Return unto Me, and I will forgive your iniquities and heal your backslidings.

There is no peace in the heart of the transgressor and no joy in his spirit. He who walks far from Me walks in darkness. But though you leave Me, I have not left you. With your own hands you have made for your soul a shack. I have prepared for you a mansion. You have chosen death, but I have chosen for you life in its abundance.

Do not faint, My child, and do not forsake the way of the Spirit for the way of the flesh. You need always My clear insight to recognize the devices of the enemy as he comes against you in the spirit. The temptations of the flesh are more easily recognizable than the onslaughts in the spirit, because the flesh is tempted to overt sin, but the spirit is the battleground of conflicts not only hidden to the outer, but all too often obscured from the scrutiny of your own spirit. Only My Holy Spirit ministering through My Word brings insight. Here only lies your security and peace.

Self-knowledge is a futile search, for man has not the key to his own castle. The mystery of righteousness is revealed only in the white light of My Word and My Spirit. I alone hold the key to inner wisdom, and I open the doors of your understanding.

Be still in My presence. Let Me minister to you in stillness, and do not fear or run from My disciplines. They are inescapable.

EPHESIANS 6:12

123

Perseverance, *the* Angel of Love

Perseverance is the rope that ties the soul to the doorpost of heaven. Without it even the most pious will fail. With it, the most stupid attain.

Not to give up in face of the impossible is your ultimate salvation. It is well called "the perseverance of the saints," for it requires saintly determination to continue on in dedication when all the forces of hell are arrayed against the soul.

Without perseverance the most beautiful life may end in shipwreck. Perseverance is to the human spirit what the rudder is to a ship. It will hold the course and steady the vessel. It will steer the ship dead ahead in spite of the contrary wind.

This you must have, My child. . .not fleshly zeal, but holy determination, pressing on in defiance of all odds. Wind or weather, friends or enemies—let nothing hold you back. There is a course to run and it has an end. To stop sooner is to forfeit it all. You will not receive a lesser reward: You will lose everything. You will not be mildly disappointed: You will be stripped naked, robbed, and left for dead.

The devil plays for keeps, and he is a ruthless master, demanding all and rewarding with death. Enter not into his evil game. If he cannot dissuade a man from following God, he will tempt him to sit down in the middle of the path, and while he takes his rest he will fall upon him and destroy him. The man who refuses to stop for rest is the one who has learned perseverance. That man will eventually reach the gate, and he will have a joyful entrance.

God's presence will be his reward. All else he has already left behind.

God's love will be his consolation. All else that appeared to have been love was but a reflection of His own.

Heaven's joy will be his delight. He has long since renounced worldly pleasure.

His friends he is with, for he has cultivated only those of like spirit.

Nothing will he miss of earth's treasure, for he has already freed his soul from bondage to material riches.

His soul is liberated into the freedom of heaven as a bird is loosed to the open skies.

And what brought him to this point? It was *perseverance*. . . that angel of holy love that prodded his soul through all the impossible situations and challenges of life. Perseverance, that blind-to-pain, dead-to-danger, unrelenting companion that would not let him go until he had received his blessing.

This man shall eventually pass through the wicket gate at the end of the highroad of absolute surrender.

OUTFLOW

Blessings are released when the soul of a man is content with nothing of earthly value. The spirit is prepared for worldly success only after it has learned to care nothing for it. I fill the hand that lies open in worship. The hand that grasps shall be forever empty.

Learn to leave to My love and wisdom all your destiny. Nothing ought concern you but the health of your soul and the outflow of your life. Man looks upon the income. I watch for

the outflow. You will free your soul as you refuse to seek anything and desire only to give. Then shall I bless you with
increase and only then will it not impoverish your spirit.

MATTHEW 16:26

THE HIGHROAD of ABSOLUTE SURRENDER

My little one, come close to Me. I have consolations for
your soul that surpass your sharpest grief. I have walked through
the deepest waters, and I am with you as you experience your
baptism of sorrow. It is the path that leads to the gate of glory,
and the Father waits to greet you there. It is not heaven of
which I speak. It is a blessedness of spirit which is given to
those who have passed through tribulations, have washed their
robes, and have set their feet on the highroad of absolute surrender. From this place there is no turning back. Having passed this
point, there is no way to retreat.

Nothing whatever that may be demanded daunts the totally
committed. It is the Father's good pleasure to give you the kingdom. Boundless is His love, and with great tenderness, He woos
you into a place of favoritism. It may cost you all, but you cannot fathom what He has in store for you.

Hold fast to His hand. He will not lead anywhere except He
be present all the time and all the way. Blessed fellowship and
holy comfort!

LUKE 12:32-40

MORNING MEDITATION

Which shall I choose today,
The hard or easy way;

To seek some soul to bless,
Or stay in idleness;

For some cause sacrifice,
Or simply close my eyes;

Work out God's thought in me,
Or set my passions free;

Seek from my foe his peace,
Or let my wrath increase;

Climb upward on my knees,
Or only seek for ease;

Give till I feel it hurt,
Or hoard the yellow dirt;

Walk where martyrs trod,
Or scorn the claims of God?

Lord, in my heart today
I give Thee right of way.

Work both to will and do,
And help me to be true.

AUTHOR UNKNOWN

Other books by

FRANCES J. ROBERTS

COME AWAY
My BELOVED
ISBN 1-59310-022-1

DIALOGUES *with* GOD
ISBN 1-59310-292-5

PROGRESS *of*
ANOTHER PILGRIM
ISBN 1-59310-291-7

MAKE HASTE *My* BELOVED
ISBN 1-59310-290-9

Available from Barbour Publishing,
wherever books are sold.